IN THE KEY

–of–

M

IN THE KEY

—of—

M

My Life, Lineage and Legacy as a Musical Evangelist

BY

WALTER T. RICHARDSON

Address inquiries to the publisher:
Allwrite Publishing
P.O. Box 1071
Atlanta, GA 30301

Learn more about the author at

ISBN: 978-1-941716-09-0 (hardback)
ISBN: 978-1-941716-17-5 (paperback)
ISBN: 978-1-941716-11-3 (ebook)

Library of Congress Control Number: 2022061909

Printed in the United States of America

DEDICATION

In Memory of Elder Thomas James Richardson
Some Minister. Some Musician. Some Mentor. Some Man.

ACKNOWLEDGMENTS

For more than 10 years, my family and I have spoken about and compiled information for use in a publication just like this that would be broadcast at some time and point. This is the time.

My wife has allowed me the freedom to think freely without clamor, to write endlessly without interruption, and to emote without fear of embarrassment. She seldom interrupts me when she's aware that I'm in *the moment*.

My mother, who flew away October 12, 1996, clipped and preserved many articles, saved pictures and artifacts, and told me many stories. I fondly recall each piece of her collection and tearfully rejoice her recollections. Her words, work, and worth are sprinkled throughout this book.

My father took many pictures, which told the stories of his life as a fourth-generation preacher's kid. He also told many stories, mostly from the pulpit, that I remember and have mentioned in this volume.

My children, grandchildren, and great-grandchildren continue to inspire and enliven me.

My aunt, Mildred Richardson, saved everything from family relics, artwork, dishes, coins, and left them for her nieces and nephews.

My aunt Nannie Rachel Richardson Liston was the family historian, having gathered family photos, obituaries, and programs which she kept in the family room in protective sheets within four four-inch 3-ring binders.

My brother, Alfred James Richardson, has been a great source of encouragement and inspiration. He has worked behind the scenes in providing me the moral courage and fortitude to fight unjust systems.

My church memberships at the Church of God Tabernacle (Miami, Florida), Hinsley Temple Church of God in Christ (Atlanta, Georgia), Second Baptist Church (Richmond Heights, Florida), and Sweet Home

Missionary Baptist Church (Perrine, Florida) each provided me the opportunity to make full proof of my ministry.

My mentors in ministry, Bishop Walter H. Richardson, Rev. John A. Ferguson, Dr. Pleasant Lawson Rowe, and Rev. Arthur Jackson, Jr. who, by their example and preaching style, influenced my delivery of the Word.

The civic and fraternal organizations that I have belonged to over the past 50 years, like the Prince Hall Free and Accepted Masons (Punta Gorda, Florida), The National Association for the Advancement of Colored People (Miami, Florida), and the Omega Psi Phi Fraternity, Inc., have allowed me to grow into my role as a voice for the voiceless.

My mentors from high school, college, and church, such as Dr. Wallis Hamm Tinnie, Dr. Mercedes Iannone, Dr. Mary Carter Warren, and Coach Leroy Daniels, have always reminded me that the same number of years that separated us when I was younger still exist. But they each have acknowledged that we now learn from, and appreciate, each other.

PREFACE

Classroom one in O'Maillia Hall was completely filled with students attending the first night of class CPS 740. This was the beginning of my second pursuit of a master's degree, but this time I wanted a degree in Marriage and Family Therapy. The students, while eagerly awaiting the arrival of the professor, were engaged in spirited conversation about their expectations from the class when Dr. Barbara Buzzi entered quietly and slowly and meticulously placed her books and papers neatly on her desk. While she prepared to begin the class, the noisy conversations dropped to dead silence. She was a petite blonde, moderately adorned, and when she opened her mouth to speak had the highest pitched voice of anyone I had ever heard, and it had a nasal monotone.

She introduced herself with very basic information, and then asked each student to spend about 30 seconds giving their names, and where they had attended undergraduate school.

She smiled and thanked us for our introductions, and after reviewing the syllabus with us, she introduced a text titled *Genograms: Assessments and Intervention*. She said we had a week to purchase the book, obtain the necessary supplies, and begin creating our genograms.

Dr. Buzzi reasoned with us that we could not understand the "systems" of our future clients unless we understood our own family systems. By her definition, systems are those events that come together that make for a complete story and profile of a person. I learned that first evening that a genogram is a family diagram, or a pictorial display of a person's family relationships and medical history. It goes beyond a traditional family tree by allowing the user to visualize hereditary patterns and psychological factors that punctuate relationships. It can be used to identify repetitive patterns of behavior and to recognize hereditary tendencies.

Dr. Murray Bowen had invented the concept of the genogram as part of his family systems model in the 1970s. Genograms were later developed and popularized in clinical settings by Drs. Monica McGoldrick and Randy Gerson through the publication of the book we were assigned to read and use. Genograms are used by various groups of people in a variety of fields as medicine, psychiatry, psychology, social work, genetic research, religion, education, and many more. Some practitioners in personal and family therapy use genograms for personal records and/or to explain family dynamics to the client.

Dr. Buzzi asked us to go back in our family's history for at least three generations. Our goal in our searches of our family histories was to determine patterns of disease and social systems. I extended my search to include patterns in education and religious involvement.

I worked hard for that one week—I actually took a couple of days away from my pastoral responsibilities to begin and nearly complete the genogram of my family. I was surprised at some of the illuminating discoveries. First, I realized that I had living relatives in their 90s and 100s. Some of them were still coherent enough to speak with me as I asked questions about our family roots and previously unspoken history. This exercise began my journey into formally investigating and drafting my family history and lineage.

I said to myself, "You know what? Unless this information is documented, my family's phenomenal history will be lost." For example, I was diagnosed in March of 2017 with type 2 diabetes, and as far as I knew, I was the only one on either side of my family that had that diagnosis. Diabetes was not mentioned when I created the genogram for my family in 2010. I asked my dad, "Does anybody in our family have sugar?" (That's what they called it back in the day.) He said to me, "No, nobody in my family has sugar."

Betty, my stepmother, was listening to the conversation (she's 23 years younger than he is, with a reasonably better memory) and said, "Walter T, do you mind if I go to the kitchen and bring you something back?" I thought she was getting me something to drink. She went to the kitchen while I continued chatting with my dad and returned with some medication that had been prescribed for my dad. It was Metformin, which is the number one medicine for people who suffer from type 2 diabetes.

My daddy didn't remember, and this was when he was 93 years old. He'd already been exhibiting some signs of "forgetfulness." I found out my father was (and is) a diabetic, and I didn't know. I'm sure that other people in my family don't know, in both the Richardson and Gaddy families, and diabetes is typically congenital. Not only was I committed to knowing more, but at this point, I was going to detail it in a book that would encapsulate the five generations of relatives, especially ministers, who would shape my life and destiny.

I so marvel at the writers who have left volumes of historical information who did not possess today's technology of internet access, computers, and retrievable data from various sources. It's bewildering that, with only typewriters, many authors and historians left clear, coherent references to times long past. Personally, I kept no diaries or journals of my life until I began my studies in Marriage and Family Therapy at St. Thomas University. I thought journaling was a "girly" thing. I had relied on my memory to recall defining periods and some disruptive moments to know who I was and what my purpose in life was. Much of my history was captured by my parents in dozens of photo albums filled with hundreds of pictures that I took delight in reviewing almost every time I visited their home. My father always had a camera from the time I was small, and his camera went wherever he went. My mother stored away news articles regarding our family, and saved relics and souvenirs from the various places the family had travelled. She even saved a lock of my hair from my first haircut, wrapped it in wax paper, and secured it inside her very large family Bible. In that Bible was recorded the Gaddy family tree. Daddy also had a large family Bible of his own, but many of the fillable spaces for family history were empty.

In fact, I noticed that every Bible for almost every black family had a family tree in the front pages before the table of contents. You know that big Bible that lay on the coffee table in the living room area of the house? But even with the photos, the relics, the family Bibles, and the coded conversations during family reunions, I didn't have a clear or complete picture of who I was, or how my life followed a pattern from previous generations.

I knew most of my family on my father's side, the Richardsons (grandfather) and the Masks (grandmother), but I knew very little about my mother's side of my family, the McLaughlins and Gaddys. As I began my research, it was clear after just a few hours that there were several things that were consistent in both family groups. There were generations, going back to slavery, of honest, law-abiding, hard-working people. It was also consistent on both sides of the family that everyone was deeply religious. The Richardsons and Masks were mostly Baptists. The McLaughlin-Gaddy side of the family were mostly members of the AME Zion Church. In fact, church life was the center of my family experience, and it remains that way today.

Now, I don't recall the word *ministry* being used in any settings of my early days in the church and around my family. In the Baptist church, there were auxiliaries, departments, and boards, and some leaders were referred to as deacons and trustees. The main leaders of the Baptist churches were the pastors, referred to as "reverends." In my home church, there were no deacons or trustees, but there were preachers who were referred to as "evangelists," and then there was the pastor. Those words *minister* and *ministry* were not used as any part of my engagement with the black church vernacular until around the 1970s.

The Reverend John A. Ferguson invited me to be his minister of music at Second Baptist Church in the late '70s. Before I said yes, I did some research and came to understand that the church had many, varied ways of serving God's people besides the choir and the ushers. I learned that there were actual ministries in the church and that, as varied as the people were in the church, there were concomitant ministries to accommodate the members' needs. For example, there is the ministry of the Word in evangelism, which affects founding and guiding churches to develop evangelists and teachers. The ministry of healing involves workers of miracles and counselors. The ministry of leadership and administration has become the new name for those in leadership over time, rather than the traditional corporate term "boards."

Church life and ministry work have shaped my personal outlook and perception about American society, as well as humanity at large. Being in ministry has influenced almost every major decision in my life, including career, marriage, civic involvement, and social affiliations. So, whether I'm playing the black and white keys on the organ or piano, or whether I'm speaking to black or white people about ways we can all conform to the image of Christ, ministry underscores the very theme of my life and now this book. My life, in fact, has been played in a particular key, which I like to refer to as "the key of M." The pitch of my story has been a resounding note related to music, ministry and management.

TABLE OF CONTENTS

1

The world I live in now compared to the world I was born into seems like two distinct sociopolitical realms for blacks. I saw society evolve from all-black neighborhoods, schools, drug stores, police departments, and restaurants to fully integrated metropolitan cities.

I lived through the development of the hydrogen bombs and nuclear weapons of mass destruction, the Cold War with Russia, the Korean conflict, the migration of African Americans from the southern states to the urban centers of the North, and the mid-20th century civil rights movement, which included the 1954 Supreme Court decision of *Brown v. Board of Education*. I saw the fall of Jim Crow, and I knew of the savage murder of Emmett Till in the past and Trayvon Martin in recent history. Residing in South Florida, I experienced the Cuban Revolution of 1959 and witnessed the displacement of jobs held by blacks and given to Cubans. I witnessed the landing of human beings on the moon and served my country during the Vietnam War. I witnessed the war on poverty, the war on drugs, the programs of the Great Society, the turbulent 1960s, the development of the pill and the sexual revolution, the inward turn of the 1970s, the rise of the mid-20th century feminist movement, the assassinations of Malcolm X, John F. Kennedy, Martin Luther King, Jr., Robert F. Kennedy, and the massacre at Jonestown in 1978. I beheld the election of the first black president of the United States, Barack Obama, as well as the change in the country's attitudes towards women and gay people.

On a personal level, I've experienced incidents of racism since I was old enough to remember. Standing with my mother at age 4 on the bus, I feared for our safety while whites looked at us in disgust. I also recall spending the night with my parents at a "transit house" in Jacksonville because our car was involved in an accident, and blacks could not spend the night at hotels. I was just 5 years old when a little white girl who peered at me through her window called me "nigger." I was trying on clothes at age 7 in the aisles of the boy's department of Sears because the dressing rooms were off limits to us. At age 21, I recall being called "boy" as I worked as a forest ranger in lieu of military service in Punta Gorda.

All along, I remained optimistic, believing that good would persist, grace would prevail, and God would provide. He did provide as I persisted. I witnessed unprecedented economic, social and political changes and was directly involved in some of it in south Florida. Meanwhile, my commitment to speaking my mind and heart ushered me into many firsts, including:

- First colored salesman on the first floor of the old Sears, Roebuck & Company, located on 1300 Biscayne Boulevard, Miami, Florida, 1966
- First black to work in the advertising department for Southern Group of Sears located in the Group or management Offices for the Southern, 1968
- First black police chaplain to serve the Miami-Dade police Department, 1989
- First black member of the Board of Directors for Habitat for Humanity, 1989
- First Minister of Music, Second Baptist Church, 1977
- First Minister of Education, Second Baptist Church, 1981
- First non-Catholic to teach religion at St. Thomas University
- First black to teach religion at St. Thomas University
- First black president of the YMCA located in South Miami-Dade, Florida in 2002

Being the first in these instances has been both a privilege and an encumbrance, as there was no blueprint to model or provide guidance. I had to learn quickly, adjust routinely, and persist relentlessly. In staying the course, as they say, I have been able to open doors for other minorities such that more leeway could be made in the fight for social and civic justice.

While I wasn't always the first black member or leader in key civic roles, I was, on many occasions, the *only* black participant. This included my role on the Miami-Dade Community Relations Board, where I got my first major taste of civic responsibility and what would become my ongoing mission to uplift and enhance impoverished, segregated communities. Inspired by that role, I founded the West Perrine Christian Association in 1989 to be able to enhance the residents' lives of the West Perrine community.

Being the founder, the first, or the only person of color within influential organizations throughout Miami-Dade County has been the hallmark of my career. From my youth, God prepared me for these roles, which I have cherished and tried to expand the opportunities for the next generation of African-American leaders. I've not been perfect, but I've tried to do my best in representing my family, community and father on Earth and in Heaven.

2

B orn into slavery in South Carolina in May 1811, Colman Gaddy's main job was to impregnate other slaves. Colman was my great-great-grandfather, who worked for the Gaddy family on their plantation in Wadesboro, N.C. He was strong and muscular, standing approximately 6 feett 9 inches, so the slave masters used him to breed. Supposedly, the slave owners used him to father children so that the prospects of having a strong, physically fit population of future slaves was secure. He purportedly fathered 45 children in South Carolina. Some of the siblings whom Colman sired moved to North Carolina in 1898, and one sister had a set of twin boys named Christopher and Columbus. These were just some of the relatives from the Gaddy lineage that our family distinctly knew of as the years passed and relatives continued to spread out across the country.

In the summer of 1943, several members of the Gaddy family met in Wadesboro, N.C., for its first formal family reunion. Since 1881, family members from Anson County and those who had relocated to other parts of North Carolina would gather to attend church, visit the family plot and local family homes. These informal yearly gatherings were loosely organized but usually involved a church worship service at the East Rock Ford Baptist Church.

The city of Rock Ford was established on White Store Road between Culpepper and Gould Fork Creeks. Community members decided not to "ford" (forge), as they would say, the creeks and, therefore, settled on either side. Those west of the creek built a church named West Rock Ford Missionary Baptist. Those to the east built what became East Rock Ford

Missionary Baptist Church in 1896. Reverend W. K. Bennett of Bennetts-ville, S.C., was the pastor who organized the church and served for several years.[1] The charter members were: Ben Tillman, John Martin, Ezekiel H. Martin, Elijah Gaddy, Dan Tillman, Lewis Caraway, Sr., Marie Hammond, Ros Horne, Malinda Pemmington, Jessie Sturdivant, Sofronia Sturdivant, Jake and Margaret Hammond, Disley Chambers, George Glake, Charity Lilly, Henry Crawford, Phyllis Brooks, Lizzie Boggan, George Tanner, Mitt Lomax, James Gaddy, Blanche Gaddy, and Colman along with his wife, Charlotte, whom he married in 1866.

By the time of the first official Gaddy family reunion in 1943, Colman had somewhat of a legendary life story. When discussing him, oral rec-ollections, historical incidents, and documented references intersected and sometimes collided at the reunion. The older members of the family remembered Colman as a tall, dark-skinned, muscular man. When he died in May 1903, his casket and grave were larger than normal. Most legendary, though, was his having fathered children from both black and white women. He had about 14 children with his wife. Some of those who gathered in 1943 were Colman and Charlotte's grandchildren. From the second generation of Gaddys, Henry and Ella were there with their 12 children[2,3]. My maternal grandmother, Roxie Gaddy McLaughlin, the third oldest daughter of Henry and Ella Gaddy's children, was present along with her children, who were my uncles and aunts. Only my uncle Howard was not in attendance, since he died the year before serving in the army during World War II.

The Gaddy family was devoutly religious. Although they had their beginnings at East Rock Ford Missionary Baptist Church, not all the

---

1   Lydia B. Bennett, Member of East Rock Ford Missionary Baptist Church from the book: "Anson County Heritage North Carolina 1995," Don Mills, Inc. & the Anson County Heritage Book Committee, pg. 42. Anson County Public Library and Union County Library Room.

2   "North Carolina, Freedman's Bureau Assistant Commissioner Records, 1862-1870," database with images, *FamilySearch*, Colman Gaddy, 21 Apr 1868; citing NARA microfilm publication M843 (Washington, D.C). National Archives and Records Administration

3   1870 Census

In the Key of M

ensuing families remained Baptist, which meant they believed that baptism should be done by immersion rather than sprinkling or pouring of water. My grandmother Roxie was a Baptist until she and her children moved to Albemarle, N.C., about 29 miles away and became members of the Union Chapel African Methodist Episcopal Zion Church. My mother, Poseline, sang in the choir and was very much involved in the Sunday school. She was known for having a beautiful, operatic soprano voice, singing not only at church but also at Kingville High School.

Although my grandmother's maiden name was Gaddy, her last name changed when she married a man from Richmond, Virginia, whose last name was McLaughlin. His nickname was "Buck," and he left the family upon the announcement of the birth of his last child. My mother told me when he came home and saw all the people at his house and asked what was happening, they told him he was a proud father again. He told the people "I'll be right back," but he was never heard from again. That happened in 1927.

Some of Grandma Roxie's siblings also lived in a small community in Albemarle named Colored Town, and each of them became members of different churches. Aunt Cora belonged to Zion Baptist Church. Uncle Charles was a dutiful member and officer at Saints Delight Holiness Church, and he went to the church almost daily, walking about half a mile to "go up there and do something." He'd get dressed in his starched and ironed white shirt, nice slacks and spit-shined, black Stacy Adams shoes and would walk up to the church. Uncle Charlie "Christopher" Gaddy was married to a very colorful, animated woman we called "Aunt Lottie." She was enamored with her television and watched her "stories" every day. Uncle Charles and Momma Lottie kept a very modest wood-framed home on the corner by Zion Baptist Church. Charles had a twin brother named Columbus, and he lived on the main drag in Colored Town. We seldom got a chance to go inside his house, and I never figured out why.

My mother was born in Wadesboro, N.C., on December 13, 1925, but she was raised in Albemarle, as the youngest girl of five children. I never met most of her siblings, and very few people in Albemarle ever mentioned her brothers and sisters except Thelma and Hattie. Thelma had one son, Edward, who was several years older than I. He was a "bad" boy and was always in trouble with the law. He ended up spending time in prison, and after his release, he was unable to find work in North Carolina. At one point, he moved in with us at our house in Opa-locka, Florida. He got a job washing dishes at a restaurant and worked until late in the evening. My daddy would take him to work and pick him up because he had no other means of transportation. My mother loved that boy almost as much as she loved me and my brother, but he began messing up again. He apparently stole things from my dad, did not obey our house rules, and then lost his job. I don't know how or when he left, but his departure from our house was swift, smooth, and unannounced. Supposedly, at my mother's expense, he returned to North Carolina and was rarely heard from except when he would occasionally write my mom for money.

I never really spent a lot of time with Edward or any of my cousins on my mother's side except for Mary Gaddy Brigham's children. She had 11 children, and they would visit us during the summers. When our family would visit North Carolina during the summer, my brother and I would spend part of the weekend with our folks from the Gaddy side, including Mary. Jimmie Brigham was a couple of years ahead of me and did not play with us, but Woodrow, whom we called "Woody," and Ronald Brigham would play with me and my brother. Tiforia, the oldest girl, wanted to play with us, but her mom and my mom forbade girls from playing with the boys. We were too rough, and our mothers didn't want to take the chance that the boys may touch the girls in the wrong place or hurt them while playing ball. We did, however, play hopscotch and jump rope together.

Regardless of the time of year or reason, my mother, Poseline Richardson, always found a way to get to Albemarle. She seldom spent time in Wadesboro with the Richardsons, even during their family reunion occasions because she did not mix well with them. She said that the Richardsons were uppity and color struck, and she didn't feel welcome at the family gatherings. Besides, Walter Harris, my dad, was the baby boy, and they made him feel very special when he was "home." They seemed to forget that he was married with children.

One of my mother's favorite relatives was Bishop James Gaddy, one of Colman Gaddy's grandsons. Bishop Gaddy was born in 1894 and entered the ministry in 1921 or earlier. He served as pastor of several churches, including Ramsey's Chapel where he was a member. His 1966 funeral program read:

In1943, he was appointed as Bishop of the "Church of God Founded by Jesus Christ" throughout several states and was crowned Bishop in 1944 by Bishop McKinley Smith. He served faithfully until he became disabled and could not carry out his duties. One of the most outstanding activities in which he took a leading part was the celebration of the General Assembly's 50th anniversary [in] September [1965].

When Bishop Gaddy realized that he would not get out again, he called in the church officials and turned over everything pertaining to the church with prayers and hopes that God's work would continue. So he moved on Saturday, February 26, 1966, at 8:30 a.m. to take up residence elsewhere. Bishop Gaddy was first married to the late Miss Minnie Chambers. To this union, seven children were born; two of whom preceded him in his death. Later in life, he married Sara Bennett, the daughter of the late Paul and Gathern Bennett. He and Sara had five children, including three daughters: Girtherine Smith of the Bronx, N.Y., Della Gaddy of New York City, Maggie Edwards of Brooklyn, N. Y., and two sons: George Pearl Gaddy of Brooklyn, N.Y., and Elder Robert D. Gaddy.

Bishop Gaddy had one sister, Annie Martin, and one brother, Wilbert Gaddy, both of Wadesboro, N.C. Upon his death, he had ten grandchildren and five great-grandchildren. Up until today, there are Gaddys all over North Carolina and beyond, both black and white. I'm sure Colman Gaddy is connected biologically to many of them.

Most of the older Gaddys walked as if they had stiff necks, which I thought was rather neat and cool. None of them, to my knowledge, completed their high school education, but many could read and were blessed with "mother wit." My mother graduated from Kingville[4] High

---

4   (The following information is excerpted from the National Register of Historic Places Registration Form for Albemarle Graded School — Central Elementary School)

The Rosenwald Fund, a national philanthropic organization devoted to erecting educational buildings for Southern African American children, subsidized the completion of six one-story, gable-roofed, weatherboarded schools in Stanly County during the 1920s. Beginning in 1921, Albemarle's African-American youth attended Kingville School, which, although located on the south edge of town, was operated by the county school system. The campus initially comprised three classrooms, with a fourth added in 1922

School in 1943 as the valedictorian of her small class. She played basketball and received a scholarship to play ball in college, but she met a young man from Wadesboro, Walter Harris Richardson, who was working in the area and they fell in love.

and a teachers' home the following year. Albemarle contractors finished the one-story brick West Elementary School for white students and the one-story brick Kingville Elementary School to serve African-American students in 1937.

3

THE RICHARDSON S

My earliest recollections of my dad's birthplace, Ansonville, N.C., was the farming area in the back of the family home. There was a barn with stacks of firewood and rusty equipment, along with chickens, a cow, a mule, and grunting hogs. I can still vividly remember the lingering smell and sounds of the farm. There were watermelons, peaches, small apples, and chinaberries. My father, Walter Harris Richardson, had nine siblings and was the youngest boy. Born in January 1923, he got his first name from my grandmother Ollie's brother named Walter Maske. Only one of my father's sisters had children, but my Uncle Amos was the only son who did not have children. Uncle Fet, whose actual name was David Lafayette McLendon, Sr., and Aunt Tinnie (pronounced "tiny") lived directly across the street from my grandparents, and they were share-croppers as well.

The Richardson family had keen, distinct features, including their above-average height, typically over 6 feet for the males. Our grandparents were all tall and had narrow feet. My father is 6 feet 3 inches and wears a size 13 shoe, and I am the same height and have the same shoe size. My younger brother, Alfred, is 6 feet 5 inches and wears size 13 shoes. My father's oldest sister, Sadie, was 6 feet tall, and she wore size 14 or 15 shoes. Both she and the next oldest girl, Marjorie, attended and played basketball at Winston-Salem Teacher's College. Marjorie, in fact, became the first female basketball coach at the school, which was referred to as "TC."

Sadie taught school for 45 years. After Marjorie finished coaching basketball at TC and teaching PE there, she came home and taught. Then she somehow got a grant and used it to become the first black entrepreneur of a of a service station in North Carolina. She got a contract with Esso Service Station and opened "Arrowhead Service Station" with a full-service garage. She hired white people to work for her, because she didn't want the people in the town to note that it was a black-owned business. So, she ended up working the cash register to stave off discrimination. Meanwhile, the people coming out and changing the tires, checking the oil level, cleaning the windshield, and filling the gas tank were all white. She made a lot of money because her service station was the only for nearly 25 miles. Fifteen miles north was Monroe, and 15 miles south was South Carolina. Her gas station was basically the last stop on that highway. There was a fork in the road right by her service station, so people had to get gas there, regardless.

The Richardsons were not only tall, but they were also stately beings, all of them, except for my grandfather, Frank James Richardson, who walked hunched over as if he was rushing to get to the next task. A man of very few words, he was not friendly and seldom smiled. I don't remember him calling any of his grandchildren by name or ever saying a word to the younger kids. It's almost as if we were in the way, even though we were anxious to see and learn what he was doing. He had a fast gait and never glanced to the side. He was always focused on where he was going. I don't even remember him looking my way. To my knowledge, he never knew my name. He suffered from Alzheimer's disease and later died of cancer.

My granddaddy Frank James Richardson, born in 1883, had long been the patriarch of the Richardsons by the time I came along in July 1948. His parents, brothers, and sisters except Elizabeth, had predeceased him. My grandfather's father was also named Frank. Born in 1846, he was the founder and pastor of Pleasant Hill Baptist Church in Ansonville, N.C. In 1870, the year the church was built and dedicated, the membership comprised mostly relatives, such as the McLendons and the Littles. Many of these members were recently freed from slavery in 1863 and had been given their last names by their slave owners. The photos of the Richardsons from that era show that they were tall, brown-skinned people who appeared serious, never smiling in the pictures. For two generations, they had been religious leaders in the community.

In my father's immediate family, he was the only minister. My great-grandfather Frank and his brother, my great-great-uncle, Elder Thomas James Richardson, were both church pastors. My great-grandfather Frank's dad was also a minister, or what people would call a "brush arbor minister." These were ministers who met with the slaves offsite to host their own impromptu worship services without the plantation owners' knowledge or influence. His name was also Frank, or Franklin, which was all of their official legal names. My grandfather hailed from a line of men named Frank, and he likewise named his first son, Frank. My father was named Walter, and he similarly commenced his own lineage of Walters, including me, my son and his son. Still, there are no juniors, as the middle names have gotten changed in each new generation.

After graduating from high school, my father attended North Carolina A&T to play basketball, but he ultimately returned home to work and help his siblings take care of their aging parents, Frank and Ollie Mae. He sang in a gospel quintet called "The Five Knights of Harmony," worked at several places, including Alcoa Aluminum factory and Albemarle Drugs. He also played on a semi-pro basketball team and tried boxing. He also had a keen appetite for alcohol, especially moonshine, at the time. After not settling into a steady professional routine and suffering headaches that caused him excruciating pain, he sought relief. He was saved during an outdoor prayer service under a chinaberry tree in the family's front yard. Now referred to as "Brother Walter," he stopped his old habits and even the headaches stopped. Shortly after his salvation experience, Walter Harris Richardson moved to Miami to live with his father's brother, Elder T.J. Richardson, who had begun a new church in Miami, Florida, in the Liberty City area.

In the 1940s and 1950s, Liberty City, or "Overtown," thrived as a middle-income community for African Americans, hosting several churches, hospitals, and community centers. Like the Harlem Renaissance in New York, Overtown was a hub for black entertainment during and after World War II in the Southeast. The area served as home to prominent figures such as Broadway singer Kelsey Pharr and M. Athalie Range, the first African American elected to serve on the Miami City Commission. The area was home to the popular Georgette's Tea Room House located at 2540 N.W. 51st Street, which opened in 1940. It was a 13-room home with a guest house that served as a retreat and meeting spot for community activists, socialites, and black entertainers such as Billie Holiday, Nat "King" Cole, and the Ink Spots (The New Tropic Creative Studio 2019). The 54-room Hampton House Hotel on 4240 N.W. 27th Avenue opened in 1954 as the "Social Center of the South." Notables such as Dr. Martin Luther King, Jr., and Aretha Franklin were regular guests, and boxing champion Muhammad Ali maintained residence there (Fields 2020). Many middle-income and working-class black families lived in sought-after Liberty Square, the state of Florida's first public housing project. The formerly all-white area included a cooperative store, credit union and community building (Benowitz 2020). This area would become the nurturing ground for Elder Richardson and for my family.

4

FROM THE NORTH
TO THE SOUTH

Elder Thomas James Richardson was born on March 13, 1886, in Ansonville, N.C., as the youngest son and the eighth of nine children to the Reverend Frank and Harriet Richardson. Although he was raised in a Baptist home, he converted and joined the newly organized Church of God. He met the founder of the Church of God, Bishop Ambrose J. Tomlinson, a former Quaker, and became a mentee of his. Although most of the members of the church at that time were white, Richardson moved up quickly in the Church of God organization, becoming an evangelist. Around 1919, Bishop Tomlinson invited him to plant and pastor an all-black Church of God congregation in Miami, Florida.

During the 17th General Assembly of the Church of God in Cleveland, Tennessee, in November 1922, the General Overseer, Bishop Tomlinson, and the Council appointed Elder Richardson as the First Overseer of the "Colored Work." To be an overseer of the colored work implies that there's another work and overseer out there. So, it was my father's uncle who was the first pastor to be given the responsibility of amalgamating the two communities under the banner of Church of God. He was specifically in charge of handling race problems that would emerge, and he became the first black bishop of the Church of God. That appointment was short lived because the Church of God impeached Bishop Tomlinson. The church split the following year in 1923 because the blacks were becoming too prominent in the leadership and the Church of God founder's brother had a problem with that. He thought there should be some separation. Bishop Tomlinson, in turn, immediately organized the Church of God of Prophecy in 1923.

In support of Bishop Tomlinson, Elder Richardson and his wife, Mamie, left the Church of God organization and joined the Church of God of Prophecy. However, with all the political turmoil surrounding the two organizations, Elder Richardson left the pastorate for a few years to do evangelistic work and preach "true holiness" in various cities, including his native Ansonville, N.C. He and his wife, Mamie, who was also licensed to preach, remained connected to both the Church of God and the Church of God of Prophecy, but they maintained loose ties so they could have the liberty to spread the gospel without hindrance during the 1930s.

Bishop Tomlinson died in 1943, and Elder Richardson was led by the Spirit to begin a new ministry that same year. He purchased two properties on 67th Street between 13th and 14th Avenue in Miami, Fla., right across from the Liberty City housing complex. With the assistance of some of the brothers from the Church of God of Prophecy, he built a sanctuary and a parsonage. He is remembered to have said that he wanted to work "seven more years for the girl that I love." Those who heard those words knew he was referring to the church, which he named the "Church of God Tabernacle (True Holiness)" located at 1351 N.W. 67th St. in Liberty City. Several people followed the Richardsons in this new church, including Austin Edwards, Sr., his wife and children, Sisters Dora May Alcorn, Estele Malone, Ethel Tyson, and Brother Seymour, who was one of the first to join the Church of God under Elder Richardson's pastorate in 1919.

While building the main wooden church building in 1943, Elder T. J. Richardson simultaneously began work on a two-story complex next to the church house. He said it would be the "headquarters" for the new church organization—he intended for the headquarters building to house visiting clergy, missionaries, and other guests, as well as provide housing for him and his wife. The building would feature eight bedrooms, with a large elevated front porch and an outdoor balcony of the same size. A baptismal pool was also built in the front yard of the church that resembled a grave, covered by an A-shaped wooden cover.

Before the headquarters was fully complete, Elder Richardson moved from the parsonage to the new building. Sis. Eunice Brown and her mother, Sister Clara Haywood, moved into the parsonage. The Hagins sisters,

Minnie Ruth and Queen Esther, moved from Wadesboro, N.C., to assist Elder Richardson in the new ministry. They lived in the new building. Blanche Calloway, sister of Cab Calloway, the famous black entertainer known for scat singing at the Cotton Club in Harlem, N.Y., lived in a house located next door to the Richardson property on 67th Street. This is where socialites and professionals, like Dr. Dennis Smith and Professor Daniel Francis, also lived in custom-built homes.

When my father, Walter Harris Richardson, turned 21, he was invited to spend a week with his uncle, Elder Richardson, in Miami. He arrived by train to a bustling sunny city. After a short stay, he returned to Ansonville, but he would later move back permanently to Miami after getting saved under the chinaberry tree at his home in Ansonville. My father moved to Miami in the fall of 1945 and lived with his uncle. He slept on a couch while Elder Richardson and his wife, Mamie, occupied a small bedroom. My mother moved to Miami shortly thereafter, because she was also invited to be part of the church where my great uncle was the pastor. Jobs were plentiful, so neither one of my parents would have a problem finding work. My dad lived in the parsonage, and my mother stayed at the "headquarters" with sisters Minnie Ruth and Queen Esther Hagins, the assistant to Elder Richardson and his wife, Sister Mamie Richardson.

It was said that "if you give Elder Richardson some mud, nails, and wood, he could build almost anything." After my parents married on March 13, 1946, following an evening service, he added another bedroom onto the parsonage, large enough for a small bed to accommodate the couple. Their lives became one with the church in every way. My mother had been a dedicated AME Zionist before she met my dad, and because of that deep rooted AME Zionism, being a Pentecostal was not difficult. Momma had a great singing voice and would always help with the opening songs and testimony services at our church. My dad had a life-changing experience when he became a Pentecostal. He went from being an unruly drinker to being completely ruled by his faith. Daddy became an evangelist and assisted with pulpit chores, but he really enjoyed preaching on Sunday afternoons on the streets of Liberty City. That was the church's main evangelistic outreach.

My parents eventually moved in with the Wiley family in a two-story house on 64th Street and 14th Avenue, and they stayed there until I was born. When my mother was pregnant and almost due to deliver, the physician, Dr. Sawyer, came upstairs to the house to determine whether she was ready. He determined that she needed more time. On the day I was born, my daddy owned an old Plymouth with bald tires, and he used it to take my mother to Christian hospital. On the way to the hospital, the car caught fire near one of the tires. Daddy got out of the car and beat the fire out with his hands. He then continued on to the hospital where I was born at 1:40 p.m. on July 2, 1948. The same year I was born, Elder Richardson completed the "evangelistic headquarters," a building just west of the church building and parsonage. It would become the main office for the church and provide housing for the pastor and his family, as well as guests. It had upstairs and downstairs bathrooms with a large dining room and spacious kitchen.

As soon as my mother was able, she went to work in the kitchen with Minnie Ruth Hagins at St. Mary Catholic Church. While she worked, I was cared for by Sister Eunice Brown, who was living along with her mother, Clara Hayward, in the small church parsonage. My father and mother moved from the Wiley's house to the Liberty Square Housing Projects, a one-bedroom house located at 1451 N.W. 65th Street.

Several young people, mostly teenage girls who lived in the projects and attended Dorsey High School, got saved in the late '40s. Being saved was considered the best experience one could have, and young ladies hearing the gospel accompanied by guitar sounds flowing out the open windows of the Church of God's facility were attracted to "seek the Lord." Among the early converts were Gussie Owens, Essie Nixon (Redmond), Maxine (Bullard) Edwards, and Gloria Hyler. Obadiah Coke and Caswell Larmond, two young men who moved from Jamaica to find work in Miami, were also saved and joined the church.

In 1949, following his graduation from Bible College in Oakland, California, Evangelist Joseph Wigfall preached at the Church of God Tabernacle (True Holiness), and several more people got saved. He preached again in 1950 at a tent revival held on the church's property, and many came to know the Lord. Shortly after the revival, which began in August, and seven years after the Church of God Tabernacle (True Holiness) began, Elder T. J. Richardson passed away in October 1950 at the age of 63. Evangelist Wigfall provided the eulogy at the funeral.

I was told that I was his favorite great-nephew. He would cradle me and take me around with him while my father worked. I was only 2 years old, but those scenes were embedded in my mind at his burial. He was laid to rest in a light-colored coffin, and I remember the handlers lowering his coffin with ropes into his grave. I was sitting but almost falling out my seat while intently watching what was going on during his burial. While I don't remember any specifics about his death, I do remember feeling the separation of this man from my life. His wife, Mamie, took over as pastor of the church, and my father supported her as an associate minister while still working at Sears full time.

Sis. Mamie E. Richardson was known in the Church of God organization as the "Elect Lady," the title given to pastors' wives. She was affectionately called, "Sister Mamie" and was never seen wearing anything black. She wore white dresses most of the time. She was a fiery preacher, with very piercing eyes and a peculiar spiritual presence. She was almost angelic in her demeanor and always connected her words and work to her spiritual evolution. She often recounted to the Saints how she fell into a trance early in her Christian experience and got a chance to visit hell, seeing all its darkness and disorder. As youngsters, the subject of hell as damnation for the unsaved was preached to us many times more than the joys of going to heaven for the saved.

5

SEARS, ROEBUCK AND FAMILY

My great uncle, Elder Richardson, had managed to secure a job for my father at the large four-story Sears, Roebuck & Company on 1300 Biscayne Blvd., Miami, Florida. Built in 1929, the store number was 1025. The number 1 indicated that it was a full-service store with a service station, catalog department, clothes, furniture, and appliances. The numbers 02 meant it was the second store of that size built in Florida. The number 5 indicated that it was a Florida store. The Biscayne Sears store housed the executive offices for the Southern region that included all of Sears operations from Key West, Florida, to Atlanta, Georgia.

Daddy was hired in 1945, shortly after arriving in Miami, as a maintenance porter. Because of his diligence and his uncle's influence, he was soon placed out front with the other workers as the head porter, or custodian. My daddy had his own parking spot for his new Chevrolet, and he positioned his car close to the employee entrance since he "opened" the store each day to turn on the air conditioning system and the lights. As the head porter, he arrived at work at 5 or 6 a.m., depending on the day of the week or if there were deliveries scheduled. He would turn on the escalators just before the store opened at 9:00 a.m. He had all the store's keys. He wore grey khakis, while the other porters wore beige khakis because "Walter," as he was called, was the head porter. Like his uncle who had worked at that same store years before, he was friendly and liked by everyone. He knew everyone by name, including the sales help, the delivery ramp workers, the managers, and the group employees.

His job involved supervising a full-time crew of about 20 people, each of whom had different jobs, apart from the service station because they worked separately. I learned supervisory skills and "being out front" from my dad, who, on occasion, had to pick up extra workers from Overtown to complete major maintenance assignments and bail people out of jail. One worker named Bob, who lived in Overtown, would get drunk every weekend after he got paid. I remember Bob because he was a hard worker, smiled a lot, and had six fingers on one of his hands.

Each of the sales departments in Sears had numbers, and Daddy had to memorize all the numbers because if the Operating Superintendent of the store needed maintenance, my daddy would be notified by a sound coming over the loudspeaker with two short bell sounds. I still remember the numbers assigned to the different departments:

1 = furniture, 3 = cameras and office supplies, 4 = jewelry, 5 = hearing aids, 6 = sporting goods, 7 = ladies suits, 8 = cosmetics, 9 = hardware, 11 = housewares, 14 = luggage, 15 = shoes, 17 = young ladies dresses, 18/38 = bras and girdles, 20 = sewing machines, 22 = stoves, 24 = draperies, 25/35 = sewing goods, 26 = washing machines and dryers, 27/31 = dresses, 28 = auto accessories, 30 = paint, 31 = ladies dresses, 33 = men's furnishings, 34 = lighting, 36 = sewing goods, 37 = carpets, 41 = men's work clothes, 42 = plumbing, 45 = men's suits, 46 = refrigerators, 47 = freezers, 57 = tv's, radios, 71= garden supplies, 87 = candy, 95 = tires

All the jobs for blacks were service jobs, including maids, kitchen workers, service station workers, elevator operators, and maintenance porters. Daddy would talk about how jealous the white workers were of him because he traded cars, usually Chevrolets, every two years at Don Allen Chevrolet. Once, while Daddy was on break and praying in the rec room, the Operating Superintendent came in and kicked him because there was a need for maintenance. He was constantly called "boy" by the white workers.

Women were still not a mainstay among the working class. Josie Turner outlasted all the other Negro female workers around the Biscayne store. She felt special because her husband, Johnny, bought her a nice car to drive from Opa-locka, and they lived in a nice home on the main highway on 22nd Avenue. Thus, she had a little extra pep in her step. Moe Mosely, a middle-aged white woman, worked as a competitive shopper at Sears, and she taught Daddy how to save money and invest through profit sharing.

While my daddy worked at Sears as the head custodian, he also worked for two different families on his days off. He worked for Mrs. Bosenberry, who was a retired music teacher from Indiana State University. She lived in Coral Gables, and her husband was a medical doctor. Because of her husband's health issues, they had to relocate from Indiana to Coral Gables. They wanted to spend their retirement years in South Florida, where the weather was better. Daddy worked with them on Mondays as a handyman, doing whatever they needed done both inside and outside their impressive coral-themed home. My mother worked there as well, doing the inside domestic work. During the summer, when I was out of school, I would go to work with them. Mrs. Bosenberry was actually the one that got me into classical music because she was a classical musician.

I also learned from my interaction with the Bosenberrys the difference in how blacks versus whites were treated. I noticed that I was being treated differently as a little black boy in the grocery store, where other kids were treated with a lot more respect. They had a lot more presence. My dad told me not to touch anything, while I saw these kids running all over the store, doing whatever they wanted to do without restraint.

My daddy was working for another white lady and cutting her yard one day when a little white girl next door looked out the window and saw me, shouting, "Hey, a nigger!" I think I was 5 years old. She had probably never seen a black child before in her neighborhood, and I certainly hadn't seen any white kids up until that point. It was likely a first for both of us, but she knew enough to call me a slur.

Similarly, when I would go with my dad to work at Sears, there would be times when I was somewhat of a novelty because a lot of those people had not seen a black child before in a public environment they frequented. And if they had, they probably didn't see one who carried himself like I did. My parents took good care of me, making sure I wore the best clothes and had the best of accommodations. We got our clothes from Sears Roebuck because my daddy got a 10 percent employee discount, and we wore Buster Brown shoes, which were custom-fitted, made-to-order.

Some of my father's white co-workers befriended or were friendly to me, but some of them just kind of looked at me in awe. My daddy took me to work one day, and I noticed as I began to learn to read that there were two water fountains. One said "colored" and one said "white." I went over while he wasn't looking and drank from the white water fountain. To my surprise, I discovered that the water was the same in both fountains because I drank from both. I asked him, "So what's the difference?" He had a hard time explaining to me, at my age, why there was a need to have two water fountains.

He merely replied, "Well, this one is for colored folks, and this is for whites."

That's when I started noticing on our annual trips to North Carolina, and on other trips out of town, that there were always two bathroom facilities, one for colored people and one for white people. The colored bathrooms were rarely maintained and often unsanitary. Every now and then, a sensitive white person would say something like, "You can use the other bathroom," meaning theirs. My mother was seemingly always given the option of using the restroom for whites because she was a woman. So there was some sympathy at times, but on many occasions, there was an absolute refusal altogether. "You can't use the bathroom here," a white patron would say. "You just can't do that."

On one road trip when my brother was still very young, we had an accident in Jacksonville. Because our car was not able to be immediately worked on and it was inoperable, we had to stay somewhere for the night. We couldn't stay at any of the hotels or motels, so we stayed at a house of ill repute, so to speak. We had to spend the night at a whorehouse because it was the only place that would take us. I can still remember the stench and the dirty bed that all four of us slept on together.

Whenever we traveled back and forth to North Carolina, the police always stopped us in South Carolina. It didn't matter when or what time of day we came through, when we drove through South Carolina, we would get stopped. My dad always drove a fairly new car, which he bought every other year, so perhaps the cops were curious about the ownership or registration of the vehicle. My dad would never speed, but it didn't matter—he would get stopped and questioned in South Carolina. We would get through north Florida and Georgia without incident, but once we hit South

Carolina, we would get pulled over. Very seldom, if ever, did my daddy get a ticket of any kind. I think what kept him and Mama from being handled aggressively was because they always had me in the car, and it would take a nasty person to handle a man crudely in front of his child. So, fortunately, we were stopped by the right racist. I was still very young when I became acutely aware that social life, work life, and even church life consisted of two distinctly different worlds in America.

6

CHURCH BOY

Church life was the center of my family experience, since I was born into a church family. I was raised as a small child in a church parsonage. As soon as I began to talk, I was taught church words like "amen" and "hallelujah." I learned how to shout before I got saved. I learned how to dress up for church. I even carried a little Bible and became interested in church music well before I attended public school.

My father was brought up in a Baptist Church in Ansonville, where his father was a deacon and his grandfather was the founding pastor. The Church of God taught that one could not get to heaven unless they were saved, sanctified, and filled with the Holy Ghost. They referred to the other religions as having some good teaching, but that they shied away from teaching "full" salvation. The Church of God was not only a Pentecostal church where the members spoke in tongues after receiving the Holy Ghost, but it was a Holiness church. Holiness churches taught strictly on lifestyles. One doctrine stood out and eliminated a lot of people from being a part of it, and that was the teaching on "double marriage." If a member of the church got married, they understood that God only respected the original vows, so members were not allowed to divorce. They were allowed, according to the scriptural teaching, to separate for a time so reconciliation could take place. If the "unsaved" partner pursued and obtained divorce, the "saved" member was not allowed to re-marry, even though they were legally free to do so.

The members of our congregation were called "saints," and there were certain activities and behavior that were not tolerated with the Lord's saints. The church members were not big on taking medicine because of their belief in Divine healing. Testimonies abounded about how the Lord had cured and healed many deadly sicknesses and diseases. Most notable was the testimony of Sister Eunice Brown, who testified weekly of being healed of breast cancer in the '40s. She would march around the front of the church, sometimes holding her breasts and rocking from side to side. Sister Tinnie Rivers always testified about how she was saved from alcoholism, and she would repeatedly relay the story of walking down the boulevard "staggering" from the use of alcohol. After having a spiritual experience with the Lord, she was delivered from alcoholism. Brother Tom, who later became Elder Edwards, would talk frequently about being robbed at gunpoint while he drove the city bus, and how the robber left without completing his act because of the power of God.

Like our family reunions, attending church was an endeavor to which my family was fully committed. In 1950, as a result of the street meetings attracting some interest, the Church of God Tabernacle (True Holiness) conducted a tent revival. The tent was erected next to the old wooden church building, and many high school students and some younger kids got "saved." Little Annie Francis at the age of 9 was the youngest convert, and her older sisters, Essie and Bertha, got saved as well. The Owens family got saved, which included Gladys, Gloria, and Kathleen, and their brother, Johnny. Johnny Wilson had moved from another city, and he got saved, as well as Hiawatha Hilliard, who was moving around doing odd jobs. Gloria Hyler, the valedictorian of her graduating class from Dorsey High School, got saved and that was a big deal because she was considered a leader in high school and would provide much leadership in the church. These "young saints" and many others who got saved together at the revival secured service jobs. Most of the young ladies got jobs working downtown at McCrory's, and the men waited tables at various cafeterias. Some got jobs at Sears, Roebuck & Co., where my daddy worked. No one went away to college. The church was their education, and they would learn doctrine, and get "the teaching" on Tuesday nights.

Sister Mamie was the absolute authority on all things spiritual and temporal to the small congregation. The young saints, mostly female, who were saved during the 1950 revival came from homes where their mothers were unsaved, so Sis. Mamie was their mentor. No decisions major or minor were made by the young saints without the guidance of this powerful mentor. She inspected their appearances to make sure the skirts and dresses were the proper length (nothing above the knee), whether their hair styles were presentable, and even if they were considering working at appropriate jobs. No one was allowed to work at a place that required them to join a labor union.

Church was held several times during the week, and no one missed any services. Tuesday was teaching, Thursday was preaching, and Friday was testimony service. Business meetings were held Friday nights before the fifth Sunday, which amounted to four times per year. Communion and washing of the saints' feet were held during the fifth Sunday evening services. Sunday morning was Bible class, and Sunday night was the evangelistic service where an altar call was always made. At the altar call, those who were seeking the Lord would be encouraged to "give up" to the Lord and ask the Lord to save them. I remember as a small child asking the Lord to save me. "Lord, save me. Lord save me. Lord save me," I beseeched.

Those who were saved would come to the altar for sanctification. Anyone seeking sanctification would be allowed to stand or sit after the prayer was given, and they were encouraged to praise the Lord until they received the "quickening." When the body jerked uncontrollably under the power of the Lord, the person was considered sanctified. Then there was the ultimate, or third blessing. These were those tarrying for the Holy Ghost. They would be encouraged to praise the Lord until they would speak in tongues. Speaking in tongues was the "initial evidence" that one had received the Holy Ghost (one could not say Holy "Spirit" in the '50s and '60s because those words were not in the King James Bible). And all this "seeking," singing and praising the Lord would last on Sundays until well after 10 p.m. Sometimes someone would "come close," and sometimes someone would "come through" and receive the blessing they were seeking. But always, every Sunday night, there would be an Altar Call made, and the preaching was always geared toward getting the saints "stirred up" to want to have a great spiritual experience. Lots of powder puffs were on hand and handkerchiefs were placed behind the collar to catch the sweat that would drip.

Once saved, new converts had to behave or conduct themselves as "Church of God" Christians. The women could not wear pants, open-toed shoes, or any blouse with the sleeves shorter than ¾ length. Skirts and dresses had to cover well below the knees. Stockings without seams had to be worn with dresses unless socks were worn, and women could not get their hair straightened. None of the ladies wore makeup or nail polish. No one, men or women, wore jewelry apart from watches. All were taught to dress "modestly" according to the Scriptures. No parties, dancing, gambling, drinking, smoking, or marriage after divorce was allowed. When saints got married, watches were exchanged instead of wedding rings. No one dated outside the population of the local church, and no birth control was permitted. Members of our community of faith were known as pacifists, so subsequently no men served in the military service. All those who were registered, did so as conscientious objectors. None of the saints saluted the American flag. No one voted in elections or accepted employment on jobs where union membership was expected.

Church services at the Tabernacle were held Sunday mornings at 9:30 with "songs unto the Lord." Then the Sunday School teachers would "take their places" inside the small church. The beginners' class, taught by Sis. Roxie Edwards, met in the back of the church on two benches. This class was for kindergarten-age students. Sis. Fountain was the assistant teacher, and her main job was to maintain order with the little ones, who seldom focused on the teacher. The primary class was taught by my mother, Sis. Poseline Richardson, and her assistant Sis. Ruthie Burkes. The kids were elementary school age and more orderly, and they didn't have to go to the bathroom as much. That class sat in the middle section of the church on the back two benches. The junior class was taught by Sis. Estelle Malone, and she was assisted by Sis. Essie Mae Nixon. Later Sis. Malone "left the church" and Sis. Essie became the teacher and was assisted by Sis. Mabel Phillips, who seldom said anything. Sis. Essie was always present, but usually late, which gave Sis. Mabel a chance to say a few words until Sis. Essie arrived, rushing and apologizing for being late. All the junior class students were high school junior and seniors, and they gathered on the two back benches on the other side farthest from the door of the church.

There were a lot of young people in the church during the '50s and '60s because the saints had large families. The youth took up more than half the church on Sunday mornings. The ages were amazingly similar, and as the two benches of beginners moved and were promoted to the primary level, and then to junior class status, there was always a new beginners' class ready to take their place. The students were not promoted based on any academic standard having been achieved; they were promoted based on age and grade in school. I was always at or near the head in each of my classes, and often I was treated as such. After all, the pastor was my great-aunt; the evangelist and unofficial assistant was my daddy; my godfather's wife taught me in the beginners' class; and my mother taught me in the primary class. Several of the girls in my classes could really speak well, and we got promoted together. Judy Mitchell, Brenda Turner, and Rosa Lee Nixon could make the saints happy when they spoke at the Easter and Christmas programs called "Exercises." Rudolph Turner and I shared the spotlight as the boys. We were the students who were regularly selected from the junior class to make the "presentation" to the pastor during the Exercises because we spoke "with feeling." At the end of the Christmas Exercise, the teachers presented each student with two gifts. One gift was a brown bag with nuts and fruit, usually pecans, oranges, and apples wrapped with a thin red or green ribbon. Each student was also given a large gift box, usually containing a shirt for the boys or a blouse for the girls.

I delighted in going downtown with my momma to shop for her class. Sister Burkes would get the fruit wrapped, and Momma bought the clothes, and I usually traveled and shopped with her. Most of the clothes came from Sears, since Momma could use my daddy's employee discount. Sister Mamie would reimburse the teachers for any expenses.

The tithes and offerings were kept at the "big house," and only Sister Mamie and her live-in assistant handled the church's money. I'm not aware of the church ever having a bank account. I do know that Sister Mamie washed the paper money, ironed the cleaned bills, and stored stacks of bills in a secure place at the headquarters. I know that Sister Mamie never drove, but always had that pocketbook clutched close to her when she went shopping.

Even though there were other girls in the church my age who were attractive, there were a few others that were a little older who always caught my attention. Arlene Wiggins was cute, and she would come to church with the Richmond Heights saints, along with Vera Randolph and her sisters. They spoke to the younger children, but they never took much time after church to converse with us. However, one slightly older girl really caught my eye, and because our families were very close and our parents had a lot in common, I saw her as a trusted peer. Her name was M. Dolores Turner. Her brother, Rudolph, was my actual godbrother, the first that I remember, and her younger sister, Brenda, was always with us when we played.

I thought she was the most wholesome looking girl, with the prettiest smooth skin and nice full legs, the kind that made you look twice and sometimes stare. Her speaking voice was gentle and soft, and the only time I remember her raising her voice was when, as we played church, she would shout "Jesus" while imitating a church member named Helen Williams. This young woman offered up a robust, animated praise to God that typically involved wringing her hands and shaking her head. She would shake her head so fiercely at times that her glasses would fall off. She was "in the Spirit," as we would say.

Rudolph, Brenda, and I were in the same Sunday School classes all through our formative years. Rudolph and I dressed alike on special occasions, especially on Easter. We sat next to each other in Sunday School, along with the other children who were within two or three years of each other in age. Mary Lou McDaniel was my age, and she came from a large family where she was the youngest child and the only girl. She was "smart" and was always good at giving her Easter and Christmas speeches, or "recitations" as we called them. Judy and Yvonne Mitchell were in the same class with me along with Larry Randolph. Rosa Lee Nixon was the best speaker, and she always acted like she was already "saved," even though she was not. She was just a good girl. All of us competed with each other in memorization and recitation so that the Saints could "get happy" and sometimes speak in tongues after we spoke. Aaron Nixon, Rosa's slightly older brother, was in my class, as well.

Assisted by Sister Rutha Mae Burkes, my mother taught the class below ours that included Tommie and Linda Edwards, Helen and Jerry Nixon, and Myrtis, Yvonne, and Jackie Mitchell. Sister Estelle Malone was our main teacher, and she was stern, strict and always talked to us about Hell. She was a tall, fairly thick woman with a light complexion and wavy long hair, which she always kept in a bun. For most of us children, we thought she might have been mixed, Caucasian and African American. This was always highlighted when her daughters, Alice and Amanda, would visit from California along with Amanda's children, Amanda Faye and Charles Jr. They would always come in their new station wagon. Sis. Estelle's grandchildren, Amanda Faye and Charles Jr., were in our Sunday School class, and she would always refer to her grands for answers to the Bible to show the rest of us how smart they were. The assistant teacher to our class, Sister Essie Redmond, who always talked with one hand over her mouth, wanted us to excel because her younger brother and sister were in that class.

Dolores escaped all this interaction because she was always, being three years older, in a class ahead of us. I always kept up with what she was doing at her home, at her school, and in her hobbies. I was aware that she was an outstanding Girl Scout, and she was well liked by the other boys and girls. Her older brother, Abraham Turner, Jr., did not attend church with us, but he was very protective of his sister "Minnie," which he called her.

I had a godsister whose name was Ramona. My mother and her mother were good friends. Ramona was five or six years older than I, and she was bad. She fought in school and got in trouble often. She got caught stealing and ended up going to reform school after the courts sent her there. I remember my family visiting her once at reform school. My mom and dad would always threaten me, saying, "If you misbehave, you will be just like Ramona." She got in trouble later in life and got a record. After just getting out of jail, she got a job working as a maid on Miami Beach. Apparently, she was stealing jewelry from the owners of the houses where she worked and ended up getting arrested. When she was arrested, she used Dolores' full name as her alias.

My godfather was Evangelist Austin Edwards. He was older than my daddy, so I considered him an older man. He was always nice to me in church, but I was never able to go home with him to visit. He and his wife had a lot of children, and most of them either stayed at his house or in very close proximity to his house. His children were much older than I, and all of them were active in church life. Austin Jr., Joe, Thomas, and Sam were the boys. Joe played piano, and Thomas played the guitar. Thomas was the main instrumentalist at church, particularly for shouting music. Nellie, Elizabeth, and Estherlene were the girls. Nellie was the pianist for the church, and played for all the song services and Sunday school exercises. She did not read music, but played beautifully and rhythmically in two keys, G and C. Thus, I was exposed more at church to my godbrother Thomas and godsister Nellie, than I was to their daddy.

Because my godmother Ethel had no children, she had a few of us at the church as her godchildren. Rudolph Turner and I were the same age, and we spent almost every Sunday together either at his house, my house or our godmother's apartment. She walked to church and went to work every day as a hotel chambermaid in some remote part of Miami. She had a dream when I was 4 years old that she saw me praying at the church altar, and then she saw me get up and go play the piano. She told my parents that dream and smiled broadly while sharing it, knowing she had provided the prophetic confirmation my parents sought about me.

7

MUSIC-MINDED

Pentecostal churches have always been music focused. Everyone in the congregation usually played some type of instrument, although they may have been tambourines made out of cake pans, cymbals made of pot covers, or just their hands. So, it was not unusual to attend a charismatic church worship service and see someone playing a piano or somebody strumming a guitar. In our case, at my father's church, there were three guitars, and two were acoustic. One was a steel-string guitar played by my godmother Ethel Tyson, and the other was just a regular guitar played by Eunice Brown. The electric guitar, which was amplified, was played by Tom Edwards, my godbrother. He was 20 years older than I, so as a little boy, I admired him and aspired to play at church like him one day. Tom was one of the newer guys in the church, but he had been nurtured by my great uncle who was the pastor and also played the guitar. My dad also played the guitar. In our church, the two main instruments of choice were the guitar and the piano.

Almost everyone in our congregation played an instrument. We had guys who played clarinet, and others who simply struck a triangle. Those who didn't play anything clapped their hands in rhythm, making it a very energetic, electric worship environment at church. My parents noticed that I was interested in the piano because I would take the toothpicks off the table at our house and arrange them on the couch like piano keys. The toothpicks were the white keys. My mom kept a jar with pennies in it, so I made the brown pennies the black keys on the keyboard. As my small hands ran across the makeshift keys, I would make-believe I was playing the piano, making sounds for each key as I played. When my parents saw that happening over and over again, they became inspired to develop my musical interest. At around the age of 4, Daddy started buying me toy pianos. He said, "We've got to get this boy involved in music."

My godmother Ethel's dream seemed to confirm that notion further. Once she shared that vision with my parents, they pursued getting me music lessons. At 5 years old, I was introduced to a lady named Ms. Martin, who was my first piano teacher. She lived nearby in the Liberty Square Housing Projects, where a lot of the teachers lived as well. At that time, it was common for them to live in the same community as the students. Ms. Martin's house was right around the corner from where we lived, and I would go there for lessons once a week. The lessons were expensive at 25 cents per session, which my parents couldn't afford, so my godmother Ethel paid for my lessons. We could not afford a piano, so I practiced at our next-door neighbor's, the Lassiter's, house, where they had an upright piano. Sometimes Momma would take me early up to the church so I could let my godmother hear me play. She'd smile and say, "My boy!"

I was one of Ms. Martin's youngest students, and she only took me on because my godmother insisted on it. Most of her music students were already in school. I would sit with my mother on Ms. Martin's couch, waiting to begin my lesson while she was finishing up a lesson with the student ahead of me. She did not use a music book, and only snarled loud directions about fingering. She used an 18-inch ruler to correct her students whenever they would make a mistake, and I was no exception. She would rap the thick, wooden ruler across our knuckles. I did not like her. Still, I learned my music lessons, and I was able to do okay under her tutelage. By the time I started first grade, she died, but I never learned of the cause. All I knew was that she was no longer my music teacher, and my new music teacher would be the lady who taught music at Holmes Elementary.

I was excited about being in the first grade. Holmes Elementary was a brand-new school in all-black Liberty City, with shiny Terrazzo floors, clean walkways, and brightly colored walls. The female teachers wore stockings and heels with their business dresses, and the male teachers wore suits and ties. Mrs. Pauline Dunn was dressed up every day and always had on something red. Everybody loved Mrs. Dunn. She had a soft, melodious speaking voice. The school had an upright piano in the cafetorium, the name given to the place in the school that served the dual purpose of school meetings and the place to feed staff and children. The students seldom met in the cafetorium for music, unless they were preparing for an "assembly" program.

Music was a mandatory course, so Mrs. Dunn would go to each classroom teaching students how to sing patriotic songs and play various instruments. We had bells, maracas, music sticks, and triangles. I was impressed as a 6-year-old with Mrs. Dunn, and certainly liked her a lot better than I did Ms. Martin. I told my momma that I wanted to take music lessons from Mrs. Dunn, and soon thereafter, my lessons began.

Mrs. Dunn was a celebrated musician, but I didn't know that at the time. She had a college degree in music and was a renowned church musician, often hired to play for local funerals, weddings, anniversaries, and so forth. She was a preacher's kid like me, so she may have learned by playing at church. She had pledged Delta Sigma Theta in college, and she made sure everyone saw her allegiance to the sorority. As such, she drove a red Cadillac, dyed her hair red, wore red lipstick, and painted her fingernails red. My mother impressed upon her that I needed to take lessons because my music teacher died, and she agreed to take me on as her student.

I went to her house for piano lessons each week with my mother. When we walked in for my first lesson with Ms. Dunn, we immediately noticed that the rugs in her living room were red. She represented her sorority Delta Sigma Theta all the way. Or maybe it was just the fact that she really liked the color red. We never asked about her affinity for red, but we looked forward to her sharing her obvious musical gift. She taught me again all the things I had forgotten since my lessons with Mrs. Martin, and she started teaching me the music notes from a long card placed just above the keyboard and from music books. She was my music teacher for two and a half years. We went to her house every week, and my godmother, who also played the piano and the guitar, was helping to make sure that I practiced in between my lessons.

I improved weekly, to the point where I started to play "by ear." This gift of playing the piano without benefit of written music helped me to play tunes I had learned in school and in church. I could pick out the notes from popular songs and play them back for Mrs. Dunn and my parents. Mrs. Dunn was delighted that I was learning how to read and play music, but she seemed more excited that I could play fairly well without any sheet music. My memorization also enabled me to cheat and play what I heard Mrs.

Dunn demonstrate without looking at the music. She always admonished me to read and play the music, but she was impressed that I was developing into a little church pianist.

Each music teacher had his or her own method and was able to share something different that I could adapt. Neither was better than the other, but Ms. Martin was just a little bit stricter in terms of discipline, making sure her students immediately got the lesson right. Mrs. Dunn would always demonstrate how she wanted me to play, saying, "Here's the music. I'll play it for you, and then we'll play it together." Ms. Martin was more like, "Here's the music. You play it."

Mrs. Dunn would advise, "You don't watch what I'm doing with my hands. Watch the music on the page. Get used to the sound and the music." Once she played the music by herself, then we would play together. She played an octave higher. Then she'd say, "Now you do it, by yourself."

That's how I initially learned to play and read music. It got to a point where I learned how to read so well that I didn't always need her to show me what to do. She was a very caring, patient teacher who wouldn't let me leave until I got it. She knew when my 30-minute session was done, but if I hadn't gotten it, I would have to keep going until I did. She wanted to make sure I'd learned something while I was there.

Our back door in the projects faced the back doors of the projects across the alleyway. The alleyway is where cars were parked. One of our back-door neighbors worked for Morgan Piano Company, and one Saturday my parents took me to see some used pianos. We didn't buy one right away. Our project house was too small, and the price may have been too much for my parents at that time. After all, my music lessons were costly at 50 cents a week, and the music books that I needed every time I advanced were 50 cents. My daddy was only making about $40 a week as the head custodian at Sears, and after paying tithes and giving offerings to the church, buying groceries, paying for his Chevrolet, and paying the other bills, he didn't have a lot of money left. I learned from him that he always paid himself and saved around 10% of his earnings. He was disciplined enough to give the church 10% in tithes, save 10% for himself, and live on the 80%. He did that well. So, for the time being, he did not have the money to buy a piano, but one day, he announced that he had a surprise.

8

SURVIVING THE PROJECTS

Sister Eunice was my caretaker while both of my parents worked. My father was working at Sears, and my mom was doing housework at various homes until she finally landed a good job at St. Mary's Catholic Church working in the kitchen. Finally, my parents were able to see their way clear of living in a rooming home to moving into the projects.

My first recollection of my home surroundings are the games that were played across the street from our little one-bedroom project house on 1413 N.W. 65 Street. Daddy parked his car out front on the street, like everyone who had a car, but would move it around back sometimes so the balls from the field wouldn't damage his car. He bought a new car every two years. We had a 52 Chevy and then a 54 Chevy. I'm told before I knew what cars were, that he had a 48 Chevy that was sold to him by Sis. Smith when she went blind.

Our neighbors on the right side with two bedrooms were the Lassiters. Most of their kids were older than me, but Roselyn was my peer. On the other side were the Andersons. I never got to know the other neighbors, except those "saints" from our church that lived across the street: the Owens.

My mother cut the grass because my daddy worked from early in the morning until late in the afternoon at Sears. One day, after cutting the grass with a push-mower borrowed from the leasing office of the "projects" managed by Mr. McBride, she turned the mower over to return it to the office. The blades were not supposed to rotate after the mower was turned over. So, I stuck my finger in the mower trying to help my mother, and one of the blades cut my pinky finger. I remember where we were standing, and the fast pace of events to get me assistance for my finger. Not only had my finger been cut, but a large portion of the finger had been cut off. My finger was wrapped with a penny and some bacon, and I was taken to the local clinic. Eventually a nail grew back and it now covers the portion of the finger that was cut off.

Living in the projects could be challenging at times, but I was okay for the most part. I walked to Holmes Elementary every day with Gary Cooper. I would play in the dirt in front of our place, and at times, get down on my knees to watch the work of the ants. Christmas was big in Liberty City. Most of the boys my age got cap-pistols for Christmas, and you could hear them shooting as early as 6 a.m. Many of them got cowboy outfits to match their guns. While some only got the hat and boots, others had the pants and shirts with the fringes as well. My daddy *never* bought me a play gun, a sling shot, or a knife. The church taught against that, so I could only watch the others. Neither were we allowed to have TVs in our houses. That, too, was against the teachings of the church. The only time I could spend watching TV was when the family went to North Carolina for the summer, and I would watch TV for hours and hours with them. The "big house" in North Carolina had a rotating antenna outside so we could get excellent reception on either CBS, NBC or ABC. Those were the only channels, even though late at night other UHF channels could be found by rotating the antenna.

My brother, Alfred James Richardson, was born in 1953, and Daddy celebrated the birth of his second son by buying a brand new four-door Chevrolet sedan. Now with an expanded family, we had to move to a larger place. So, we moved to 6226 N.W. 13th Court, where we rented a two-story home in the projects. The house was connected to several other homes that were either one or two bedrooms. Downstairs was the living room and kitchen, and upstairs was the bathroom and two bedrooms. My brother and I had twin beds, and my parents had a full-size bed. I never heard of queen- or king-sized beds in 1953.

Daddy kept the house nice outside. He forbade the kids who would play in the street in front of our house to ever hit a ball over to his property. We didn't have a big yard, maybe about 25 feet, but it was always cut and filled with seasonal flowers. He took great pride in his flowers, such as gladiolas, and he changed them throughout the seasons. Momma kept everything "spic and span" inside. She was always dusting. Daddy replaced the linoleum when needed and fixed all the plumbing. Cleanliness was next to godliness in our church, and the "saints" were held to high personal standards, especially in our homes. Floors were swept, kitchen and bathroom floors were mopped often, and clothes were hung up. With many members of the church working in white folks' homes as domestics, they knew and maintained the standards intrinsically. Some saints had chinaware from their boss ladies and bedspreads with little matching dolls in the middle of the bed. "What nots" were always visible. The screens were cleaned often, Venetian blinds wiped down, toilet bowls were cleaned with Ajax or Comet, and toothpicks sat in dispensers on the kitchen table. A picture of white Jesus with flowing blond hair, blue eyes and a masterfully cut beard was hung on the living room wall of many of the saints houses or apartments. We had a screen door and a regular door that got locked at night. On the back of the regular door were two nails. One held the policy for Life of Georgia and the other nail was for Independent Life. Once a week, two different white men with thick books would come by and collect money for insurance. I never understood this, but it was a way of life for my community.

All the ambulances were owned by either the Williams family, who owned the cabs, or the funeral homes. So if there was a family health emergency, one could call for one of these services. All the police officers who patrolled Liberty City were black. The only time we saw a white officer in our community was when there was a need for a police motorcycle. The motormen were always white.

We ate what mom made for dinner or we ate nothing. Dinner was served at a certain time, and we all ate around the table as a family. Sometimes our family would eat at someone else's home on Sunday afternoons, or another family would eat at our house. We never ate at restaurants or cafeterias until the early '60s, and then we ate at Toby's or Morrison's. The staple food for traveling was a bologna or peanut butter and jelly sandwich. For a special treat, either Daddy made ice cream or we would visit the new Dairy Queen, which was close to Dorsey High School. We were introduced to JELL-O at some point, and it became a regular dessert at home.

When I came home from school, the first thing I did was take my school clothes off and put on my play clothes. I had three sets of clothes. My school clothes were always khaki pants in beige or grey colors, and I wore a little belt, most of them acquired from the Seminole Indian village. The shirts I wore to school were always colored collar shirts, mostly plaid. My play clothes were jeans and old school shoes that were too small to wear to school. My church clothes were always "regular pants" in black or blue, because my momma said, "they matched everything." Momma would buy two or three sets of shirt-bowtie combinations, and then I had two or three jackets that "matched everything."

I had to do my homework before I was allowed to play. We used encyclopedias to do research for school. If we needed to talk to someone from school about anything, our circular rotary phone was next to the couch and it had a short cord. I walked four blocks from our house to Holmes Elementary School every day. When I was in second grade, sometimes I'd walk with Roselyn Lassiter, my next-door neighbor. I never got a ride to school. The only children that rode a bus to school were the special education students.

In the warm summer months, we used two electric fans, one rotating ceiling fan and another moveable floor fan. When it got cold, we had a kerosene stove, and I can remember that strange kerosene smell. I remember Daddy having to change the wick and momma setting a pot of water on the kerosene stove, but I never understood the purpose of it. People watched TV on black & white sets and had to turn the knob on the set in order to turn the channel, which were limited to major networks, such as ABC, CBS, NBC and public television. The television sat on a rolling cart, and antennas, or rabbit ears, were moved around to get better reception. The radio in our house was always tuned to WMBM, an AM station that played gospel music all day long. Milton "the butterball" Smith and Rev. Ira McCall were two of the main disc jockeys that played church music. On Saturdays, we read the funny papers or rode our bikes. We weren't afraid of anything. If someone had a fight, that's what it was and we were friends again later, if not sooner.

The kids played Mother May I, Hopscotch, Cowboys and Indians, Cops and Robbers, 1,2,3 Not It, Red Light Green Light, Red Rover, Hide & Seek, Truth or Dare, Tag, Baseball, Kickball, and Dodgeball. Girls would spend hours playing house or with their dolls. Boys played football and baseball in the street or at the school park and climbed trees. We rode bikes and would become daredevils by making a ramp with scrap wood stabilized by a rock or concrete block to jump our bikes, launching us into the air and then back to the pavement.

In the Key of M

Staying in the house was a punishment and the only thing we knew about being "bored." If we claimed or even mentioned being bored, our parents would warn, "You better find something to do before I find it for you!" When I was outside and needed to drink water, my friends and I drank from the nearest water hose. The refrigerator had a small freezer with one or two metal ice-trays. We played until it was so dark, the street-lights came on.

The growing influence of blacks migrating to South Florida from the Caribbean impacted the culture, especially in terms of food and music. A calypso band would come through Liberty City every now and then. Many times, they would not sing, just play exotic rhythms on the drums, guitars, and horns. If they had gathered a small crowd along the way, they would stop as a group at one of the project wash houses and play until everyone had to retire for bed.

The one-armed peanut man would come through the neighborhood at least once a week, normally late on Saturday afternoon, yelling, "Peanuts, hot peanuts!" He would add, "I ain't coming back tonight," so that people would have to run and catch him before he left with his little brown bags filled with warm peanuts or wait until the next week.

School was mandatory, and teachers were people whom you could trust and respect, and most of them lived in the same neighborhoods and attended the same churches. We watched our mouths around our elders because all of our aunts, uncles, grandparents, godparents, and our parents' best friends were also our parents, and you didn't want them telling your parents that you misbehaved. Paddling was common for the kids who misbehaved in school. Teachers used rulers to hit students on their hands and fingers if someone was caught doing something naughty. Essentially, everyone could (and would) whoop you.

9

SISTERHOOD OF SAINTS

Her son quickly dropped her off for every church service whether Sunday, Tuesday, Thursday, or Friday. He'd pull up to the church and leave his car running as he exited to go around to open the door for her to exit. He'd hurriedly lead her up the two steps to the church door, guide her towards her seat, then he'd leave as quickly as he dropped her off.

Sis. Minnie Smith was always seated upright in our little sanctuary, with her head forward, belching quietly when my family arrived for worship. We always arrived early, sometimes by half an hour, so my daddy could check on Sister Mamie, his aunt, next door at the parsonage. But Sister Minnie Smith always arrived much earlier. Most of the women of our church were known by just their titles and first names: Sis. Poseline was my mother, Sis. Maxine was my godbrother's wife, and Sis. Mamie was the pastor. But because of the unique qualities of the church's only physically handicapped member, everyone called her by her complete name: "Sister Minnie Smith."

She sat on the very last pew of the church in the corner next to the window. She walked armed with a cane, wore dark glasses, and never moved her head. She wore perfume that smelled dated to me. She testified on Friday nights and always sang her favorite song, "Reading that letter… all night!" Sis. Minnie Smith did not smile and was considered a "mean" woman by the children of the church. We'd laugh about her favorite song, talking about "reading" when we all knew she could not read.

We held our Sunday school class in the same corner of the church where she sat, and she did not change her seat to make room for the students. Nobody dared suggest that she should move. The students would stare at her as she guarded her cane and clutched her tambourine. She carried a black purse that she opened at offering time to contribute a quarter. She was a cherished member of the church, having joined when the church started in that location in 1943. When my dad moved to Miami in 1944, he purchased his first car from Sis. Minnie Smith, a 1927 Ford Model-A with a rumble seat. I never knew how she lost her sight, but it had not been that long since she went blind.

My dad often travelled with Sister Mamie when she visited different sites and cities to evangelize. One weekend, my mother tagged along, and they took my little brother, who was about 4 at that time. Unbeknownst to me, my momma had asked Sis. Minnie Smith to keep me overnight.

I walked three blocks home from Holmes Elementary School that Friday, and Momma told me, as she lovingly placed her hands on my shoulders, that I would be staying overnight with Sis. Minnie Smith. I was anxious and she knew it. However, she also knew that this experience would not be harmful to my psyche. Before the sun went down, my parents drove me over to her green wood-framed house located on the very busy corner of 65th Street and 17th Avenue. We had passed by her house many times, but I had never seen it up close. Like a sniper looking for targets, I immediately noticed that there were no flowers or bushes, and the short patches of grass mixed with hardened dirt were guarded by a faded chain-link fence. The side door off the front porch was wrapped with closed aluminum shutters.

My momma escorted me up to the side door of her house. Expecting us, Sis. Minnie Smith met us at the side door before we had a chance to knock. She invited us in, and then after my mother gave her my food for the night and shared a few brief words, Momma departed with my daddy and little brother into the fading sun.

Sis. Minnie Smith sensed my discomfort because the house was eerily but necessarily dark, and I froze on the porch, glad to see the remaining sunlight that was sneaking through the shutters. She sat down in a wooden chair on the porch near me and quickly asked me what grade I was in at school and how I was doing. My voice quivering, I told her that I was making all E's (Excellent) and S's (Satisfactory). She then asked me if I knew my ABC's, and because I knew she could not see me, I stuck out my tongue at her. I had learned my ABC's in kindergarten.

"Yes ma'am, I know my ABC's," I responded with arrogant shyness.

She asked me then to sing my ABC's.

I sang, "A-B-C-D-E-F-G, H-I-J-K-LMNOP."

She said, with a slightly raised voice, "Start over and go one at a time."

I waited for a second before I began again. Those seconds felt like minutes, and I sheepishly said "A."

She said, "As for me and my house, we will serve the Lord."

I said "B," and before the B sounded faded, she interrupted by saying, "I'm not through with 'A' yet. 'Ask and it shall be given, seek and ye shall find, knock and the door shall be opened.' Now, go ahead."

I was understandably terrified, but I was impressed with her rhetorical ability. I quickly remembered that she had been a guest at several dinners after church at different saints' homes. When we went around the table holding hands following the grace and everyone was required to recite a memory verse, Sis. Minnie Smith always had a different Bible verse to recite. I smiled as I remembered that. For "B," she said, "Believe on the Lord Jesus Christ and thou shall be saved."

I said "C," and she responded, "Come unto me all ye that labor and are heavy laden, and I will give you rest."

This back and forth went on until we covered all the letters in the alphabet. I was sleepy following this exchange, and I don't remember eating dinner or when I went to bed. I never forgot my alphabetical recitation of verses after that Friday night experience. I felt like I was really a church boy after I began then to master recitation!

To facilitate mastering scripture recitation, I started reading my Bible a lot more, especially every time I went to the bathroom. My daddy gave me a small, used, green-zippered miniature New Testament, which included the Psalms and the book of Proverbs. I began carrying it like a knife in my back pocket and would whip it out to check my accuracy in recitation. I carried that little Testament all the way through elementary school and on through high school. Since I was really skinny, I also carried a little wallet with my school patrol picture in it. I always had at least a dollar, and I proudly kept my wallet in my right back pocket and my Bible in the left.

I started looking and listening at what was being said in church. There were four activities that involved someone speaking: exhortation (the introduction), teaching (by the pastor and Sunday school teachers), testifying (saints), and preaching (evangelists). The differences between these four activities were subtle, and they each involved the Bible. Those that exhorted on Tuesday nights behind the table used the Bible to read or quote scripture to encourage the saints and others to live out their faith in their homes, with their families and friends, and in their jobs. The teaching that was done by the pastor used some of the same scriptures, but the presentation was more doctrinal and denominational. The Sunday school was divided into three age groups. The beginners' class was for children up to 6 years of age. They learned that Jesus loves them, and they learned some very short Bible verses. On Friday nights, the saints would testify and give accounts of recent experiences where their faith paid off, or they would recall old familiar stories of how they were healed, set free, or delivered from sin. There was teaching and then there was preaching. To me, the difference was that teaching involved repeating scriptures and stories so that the children could learn, memorize, and repeat what had been said. Preaching was reciting those same verses in a rhythmic way, enough to get the saints and congregation excited enough to either cry and groan aloud or to jump up and say amen.

My inclination toward learning Scripture was reinforced during Saturday Bible Class at the Laundromat, or "wash house." The young kids from the Church of God would gather around at noon to sit on the steps of the wash house located on 67th street, near 12th avenue. One of the young saints, Sister Gloria Hyler, would teach us songs and key Bible verses. The B-I-B-L-E song was my favorite. The teacher did not have to encourage us to stand and move for this song. We had broad smiles and were loud and enthusiastic when we sang the lyrics:

The B-I-B-L-E, that is the book for me
I stand along with the Word of God,
The B-I-B-L-E.
God's word will never fail, never fail, never fail
God's word will never fail, NO, NO, NO!

"Jesus Loves the Little Children of the World" was another favorite, and memorable to this day. We would recite all the books of the Bible. In the Old Testament recitations, we shouted out the books loudly until we got to the prophets, then our voices dropped as we slowed to pronounce the unusual names, such as Habakkuk.

Most of these instructional activities, including preaching, were led by women. Some would consider a Pentecostal church to be too conservative to advance or include women, but that was certainly not the case at our church. All decisions were made by the pastor, Sis Mamie. She was consulted before any saints made major purchases, such as homes, apartments, or cars. She had to approve of all marriages, and even who would be the new members of the church. She was a short woman with Native American features and complexion, and she never drove. We, or other church members, drove her everywhere she needed to go.

Most of my teachings about life came from the women in my family, church, and community. My mother was my primary teacher, teaching me as a child how to bathe, brush my teeth, hold a fork, and use a toothpick. I learned my alphabet from my kindergarten teacher, who was a tall, thin, pretty woman of about my mother's age. Ms. Martin, an older woman, probably in her 40's, was my first piano teacher. Sis. Roxanne Edwards was my Sunday school teacher. Sister Eunice Brown was my babysitter when I was an infant. Sis. Hyler was my Bible class teacher on Saturdays, and all my elementary school teachers were women. Mrs. Thena Crowder was the principal at Holmes Elementary, where I attended school from the 1st through midway the 3rd grade, and Mrs. Sylvia Lambert was the principal at Bunche Park Elementary where I went after. Men were around in all of these circles, but many boys my age and I were heavily influenced by the women in our lives.

The men around me did not talk to boys much, except to bark out instructions and give directions. I think they thought it was unmanly for a man to spend time talking to or interacting with children. In my community, the men worked hard every day. My daddy left for work early in the morning, and when he "knocked-off" at 3 o'clock, he'd arrive home tired with his back hurting and feet swollen. Although he'd greet us gleefully, he didn't feel like talking. Around the time I was in the 3rd grade, he started reading, without comment, to me and my little brother from the book of Proverbs. He always read the first few verses of the fourth chapter. What he taught us, we learned from us watching him practice what he preached. And so it was, the women did most of the talking, and we watched the men.

10

M O V I N ' O N U P

S everal of the "saints" had moved from the projects and from other apartment buildings in Liberty City to own their own homes. Developments for Negros were springing up all over Dade County at the time. Several of the members of the church moved to Richmond Heights, a new development located about 30 miles south of Liberty City. Others moved to Opa-locka, located about 15 miles north of Liberty City.

School teachers, principals, and business owners lived in a special area within one mile of each other in Liberty City, but the homes were very large CBS (concrete block structure) constructions with huge lawns, plush green grass, driveways, and garages. They were always decorated nicely at Christmas time. The owners' names were always in the "Miami Times" newspaper because they were involved socially and politically in Miami and beyond. Daniel Francis and his wife, Susie West Francis, were educators; Thena Crowder was the principal of Holmes Elementary; Dennis Smith was a dentist and lived on the next corner from our church building.

Evangelist Thomas Phillip Edwards, better known then as "Brother Tom," had moved from the Lincoln Fields apartments to a home in the fairly new Bunche Park area of Opa-locka. We went to visit several places around the county to look for a home. The homes in Richmond Heights were nicely built with barrel tile roofs and carports, but the distance was too far from downtown Miami where my father worked. Opa-locka was not as far away, only 15 miles from our church in Liberty City, and only 25 miles from Sears. So Daddy visited Opa-locka, and after seeing and liking Evangelist Edward's house, he decided to investigate the possibility of purchasing a home in that area.

We moved to Opa-locka when I was in the third grade. Daddy was able to buy a house, our first. It was raggedy, with cracked floor tiles and broken windows, and it needed a paint job. I was not impressed with it until we cleaned it up and discovered it had lots of room in the back yard, an extra bedroom, and neighbors who also had houses.

Just before we moved to Opa-locka, my daddy bought me a big piano. The guy who worked at the piano company actually knew the Morgan family, who owned the company. Apparently, he told Mrs. Morgan about this young boy in his neighborhood who was learning to play the piano, so my dad got a very good deal on it. The company delivered the piano to our house in the projects. In the second semester of the third grade, we moved to Opa-locka, which is about 7 miles, or 20 minutes, from Liberty City. Nevertheless, we kept going back and forth for my music lessons, and I had a new piano on which I could practice.

During this time, I was also starting to pick up the guitar because my daddy played the guitar. Once I learned how to play the guitar, I played both instruments with about the same level of skill. Although guitar music is logged a little bit differently, I could read guitar music and piano music. I became proficient on both instruments by the time I was in the 4th grade. I began playing for people at home and church. I was being featured during school assembly programs. A couple of teachers, who were also musicians, took an interest in me. One was a guy named Eric Knight. He had originally gone to the military after he graduated college at Florida A&M University, where he was a musician. He was a jazz musician and noticed that I had talent. He asked me to stay after school one day, and I did after getting my mother's permission. He started teaching me how to play jazz, so that's how I picked up my jazz influence. From that point, I knew, and I think we all knew, music would be a significant part of my life's journey.

My first day at my new school, Bunche Park Elementary, was traumatic. My mother took me to enroll, and the kids were not nice to me in my class. I found out later from Theodore "Zack" Miller that the boys in my grade wanted to beat me up because I came from Liberty City and I carried a book bag. Either way, I was a threat to them, and they did not want me to get too comfortable. He stopped them and said, "He's probably smart and we may need him." I never had any problems after that with my homeroom class. I even became a school patrol again and was selected to make a commercial that would be shown on television. The commercial used my voice to speak about using crosswalks, and it showed me helping students across the street. I saved my school patrol identification and still have it to this day.

We had a lot of kids on our block on 18th Court. There were like 100 kids between the 20 houses, and everybody knew everybody. We were the smallest family, with only two kids. The Hannas lived across the street and there were about seven of them; all of them were older than I except Shalita, who was the same age as my brother. The Avants lived next to the Hannas, and they had eight kids. Ernest was the oldest, and then there were his two sisters, who were real fine, but ghetto, like their momma. There was always fussing and fighting going on in the house. Every day there was an argument, and I remember my momma peeping out the curtains at night watching and listening at the commotion.

The Colliers lived right next door to us, and they had nine children: seven boys and two girls, named Eugene, William, Samuel, Bubba, Hansel, Sister, Linda and the twins, Ronnie and Larry. The Jacksons lived next to the Avants, and they had ten children. Willie was the oldest, and then there were James, Nathaniel, Robert, and another brother, who was gay, and there were several girls, the oldest of whom was called "Sister." She had a birth defect, which rendered her unable to speak clearly because her mouth was permanently half-open. Surprisingly she was able to be understood, as she used her tongue to help her shape words and expressions, and she *loved* to talk.

The Crosses lived next to the Hannas on their right, and all the Crosses were heavy, except for the one girl, Betty, who was slender and beautifully bow-legged. Two Gilbert boys lived with their parents next to the Crosses. One was older than I, and the other was along with my brother. They never played with us. The Radfords lived next to the Gilberts, and they had eight kids as well. John, my classmate, was the oldest, and Paulette, one of the younger sisters, was "retarded," which we would refer to as "developmentally delayed" today. Most of the kids were afraid of her because her behavior was understandably unpredictable. The other households with kids on the block included the Barnes family, who had James and his sister, Doris. "The girls," as they were called, included four sisters who were related to Mrs.

Alberta Harris, our next-door neighbor on the left. She drove a Ford Falcon, which, along with her attractive four nieces ("the girls"), I admired at the time. The Cannons only had two girls and a boy. They, like us, were among the few smaller families in our neighborhood.

The only daddies on the block who got involved with us kids were Mr. Jackson who cut hair, and Mr. Collier who also boot-legged cutting hair on his back porch. Mr. Collier was not trained as a barber, so he nicked us often, but the haircuts were cheap and convenient. His family comprised two girls and eight boys. Their mother was sanctified, and one of the daughters, Gloria was the first one on our block to get sanctified as a child. She wore the traditional long dresses in high school with the doilies, proud of her affiliation with the sanctified church.

On a regular basis, the boys around my age would get together in the street in front of my house to play football. Willie Jackson, one of 15 kids in the Jackson family, was the assumed quarterback for one team, and John Cross was always the quarterback for the other. Willie would stack his team with his brothers and the Collier boys—they were the best athletes, and John would get the Radfords to play on his side. I would not get picked very often because I was not that tough, and my mother always cautioned me to take care of my hands because I played the piano. Most of the time, I didn't play; I just watched from my fenced-in yard.

The bathroom in our first house was the scene of some unusual activity. First there were items that took me years to understand their purpose. My daddy shaved with a very heavy razor that used a double-sided blade and screwed open and closed for operation. There was the proverbial hot water bottle that had a long cord that was used to place on our stomach when we were constipated. I was in high school before someone explained to me its real purpose, and only then, by accident, did I really understand. One of my friends had called a girl a "douche bag," and with my non-street-savvy-self, I inquired what that was. I later told my mother of that conversation, and she smiled without comment.

There was the need, it seemed fairly often, to have the septic tank at our home cleaned because dirty water and fecal matter would back up into the house from overuse of the toilet. We used baking soda and salt for toothpaste, not only because they were less expensive than toothpaste, but because the salt was more abrasive and helped remove the grime in the mouth. Besides, the baking soda helped polish the teeth to a brilliant shine. We took baths every Saturday night, and washed off several times each day. We called our washcloths "wash rags" because many times large towels, some donated, were cut into nice even pieces to make smaller towels and wash cloths to accommodate our household usage. But we were always clean. Momma made sure that Alfred and I washed everything, every day, from our faces to our feet. Vaseline was used to cover the "ash" on our arms and legs. Baking soda was used sparingly under our arms. I don't remember using lotion until I got married. Royal Crown was kept in the medicine cabinet to make our hair shine. That was the last step before being considered ready for going out in public. Momma would usually call out after Alfred and I were washed-up and dressed, "Did you all brush your hair and thing?" I never asked my mother what "thing" she was referring to, but I found out later that all of the Gaddys said the same thing to their children.

11

CIVIC AND LIFE LESSONS

Life in Miami's black community revolved around the church. One of the main questions people would want to know is if you went to church, then where you went to church, but more importantly, who is the pastor. It all focused on the church and the pastor. As such, pastors, like my uncle, served a lot of roles beyond just church functions. If someone had to go to court, the pastor always went. If they got sick, the pastor was always invited to the hospital or house, wherever the person was recuperating. If they had financial challenges, the pastor had all of the networking power necessary to get people back on track. Pastors were invited to almost every community function and program. My father was no different when he later began his ministry. He got called upon quite a bit to handle things in the community. Perhaps in other communities, religious leaders are not as pronounced as they are in the black community.

Because my father was a pastor, the spotlight was on us as a family, and there were strict social standards we had to maintain. My brother and I had to always make sure we dressed and acted appropriately. We were not given the same opportunities to get into mischief and misdeeds as some of the other kids who were also ministers' children. There was one pastor, Johnny Wilson, whose children were bad, all of them. They weren't held to the same standards as Alfred and me. We had to act like we were anointed even though, at that point, we hadn't been saved.

My parents set a clear expectation that their children were going to act the part. We were going to participate in everything positive and promising. We weren't just going to be good, we were going to be the best at everything, especially school. This was an easy role for me because I was raised to be a perfectionist, but my brother, not so much. He did things that I didn't and could not do. He didn't really get away with it, though, because he ended up paying a pretty hefty price for his misdeeds.

When my brother got out of elementary school, he started messing up a bit and doing things that he shouldn't. He wasn't doing his homework and lacked self-motivation. Seeking a change in environment, my mother wanted Alfred to attend a Christian school rather than the neighborhood public school. The school was called Dade Christian School in Miami Lakes. My dad told my mom to get in contact with the school during the summer to make sure that Alfred would be properly prepared for the seventh grade. They got all the paperwork filled out and had several phone conversations with the school to get him enrolled. When my parents took Alfred to the school and the administration saw him for the first time, they determined that they didn't have any openings. My mama figured out right away that it was because he was black. Daddy didn't believe a Christian school would discriminate based on race. Soon thereafter, he was educated and exposed to the fact of pervasive racism in the Christian community.

No matter how great the social pressure and practical responsibilities of being a first lady were, I never heard my mother complain. I never even sensed her frustration. If she did have grievances, she didn't express it in any form that I was aware of at the time. She supported my father completely and unconditionally, never getting in his way. They were comfortable as a couple, as parents, and in ministry. They did a lot of things together for the church. She was really my father's alter ego.

Half of the church community, at our local church, was children, and Momma had a major impact on them. She was major teacher in the Sunday school, and everybody had to go through her class. An excellent singer, she helped with the music and sang in the choir as the lead soprano. She was always at the church. There was never a time that she was not there.

She never had a problem with it because she understood the role of first lady after having watched my uncle's wife and how she dealt with him taking on so much responsibility. Maybe she was also comfortable in the role because she trusted her husband, so she became even more comfortable. Anytime Daddy had to go out of town for church-related work, she was right there. Very seldom did Daddy go out of town on a pastoral trip or even a family trip where she wasn't there. He did go to places without her when he was in town, but whatever he had to do, it happened in the daytime. There weren't many night visits he would ever take.

My father, like all the Richardson men in church ministry, were all approachable, sociable, and caring. As the old expression goes, my dad would give you the shirt off his back. People were drawn to him as a result, including some of the women in the church.

The whole aura of being a man of authority, especially because he was *that* pastor, is attractive. I believe my father would not have been as appealing if he did not have that title attached to his name. Some people are almost naturally attracted to religious authority figures; it puts them in a position where they can't mess up because they're connected to God in some way. They act as if there is some sort of blessing attached to being involved with a preacher.

Infidelity was pronounced in many church circles, but my father kept his focus on saving souls and supporting families. He would even go with people to help them purchase a car and help with ensuring they get proper financing, because nobody wanted to play with or mess with the pastor. "This man, he's a man of God, so we're not gonna cheat him," many people thought. This was the same mentality people had when going to court. They thought, "The judge is going to listen favorably to the pastor." Even the guilty felt that having my father there would bring special treatment. "Even though I may be guilty, I'll get more mercy because my pastor is with me," they thought. Understanding people's reliance on him, he never sought to take advantage of his standing, including financially.

Pastors always seem to have access to capital. I'm not sure how this is almost always the case, but I know how it happened in my family's instance. My great uncle taught my father about saving and tithing, which are both necessary in responsible money management. As such, my daddy had never struggled for money as a full-time pastor.

Unlike many families in my neighborhood, we could afford to travel at least once per year during the summer. In 1965, for instance, we went to the World's Fair in New York. My father's Aunt Mamie had a relative who lived in Harlem, and we went by to visit her. The apartment where this lady lived was way up on one of the floors. That's where I met a Puerto Rican girl who was about my age. I had learned to speak Spanish, so I started talking to her. The girls in New York wore jeans with bobby socks and possessed a certain liberty in their demeanor. I liked her style because it was so different from the girls back home in South Florida. While I was talking to her, this group of guys came up to me and said in Spanish, "Who are you?"

I replied, "I'm here visiting with my people."

They said, "Well, you can't talk to her."

At that moment, I had no idea who they were, but later I learned they were part of a gang. This was a first for me. I'm sure there were gangs in Miami, especially in our area, but I never knew of them. I seriously had no idea. Even though we were raised in the projects until I was in the third grade, my brother and I were shielded from the criminality and decadence. Being five years younger than I, Alfred really had no idea about what was going on outside our home or church. I heard gun shots at night, stories about people being stabbed and police sirens blaring down the street. Despite that, my parents made sure that they gave me minimal information. They did not really give me those important life lessons on how to how to act if, in fact, you were involved in "street life" situations. I was a little naïve, to say the least.

I didn't know anything about sex until I got to the seventh grade. I had no idea where babies came from, none at all. At the time, the schools weren't teaching sex education, so you had to learn from family, friends, or life itself. I saw young women getting pregnant and people in the church, but I no idea what that was all about. Then in the seventh grade, my good friend Anthony, who later became my Omega Psi Phi frat brother, started talking about the fact that he and the other boys were getting "boongy" in the sixth grade. I didn't know what a "boongy" was, and my parents never told me about my "boongies." I had no idea what a vagina was in the sixth grade. Ultimately, I came to find out that they were boning girls, which was done with all your clothes still on but in the same position. So, they *thought* that was having sex. So maybe all of us were naïve at the time.

As a little boy, the first time I saw a female baby getting her diaper changed was when I noticed the different anatomical paraphernalia in boys and girls. "What's going on here?" I mused.

Noticing my confusion, my mother explained, "You know, that's a girl. That's how you tell the difference. She has that and you have that." I've never inquired further about why that was, and that was the extent of my family discussion about the differences in males and females.

All that changed quickly in high school, where I learned everything I needed to know about the "birds and the bees." Yes, things become very clear in high school.

12

THE BIRDS AND THE BEES

Because of my dad's physical stature, he had a commanding presence, and his children had great reverence for him. In terms of his temperament, he spoke very slowly and deliberately. As a father, he was very strict and didn't have to say a lot for us to know that we needed to conform. He never had to repeat himself, because we knew he meant what he said and said what he meant. He did not punish us often, but when he did, he made up for the times that he hadn't. Although stern, he was humble and compassionate, willing to help support his family and others however he could. As a child, I may have gotten my butt beat for misdeeds, but as I got older, it was more about beating me with his mouth than it was physically. My dad had a way of keeping you occupied in conversation while making you feel bad about whatever you'd done that wasn't right.

I remember the first time he found out that I was having sex. One of the girls named Cindy from the church had gotten in trouble, and my mom recommended to her aunt that she spend a weekend with us to get away from the upheaval. Apparently, the girl was having some problems with her mom, and her aunt tried to intervene. She was an infrequent visitor at our church, so we didn't know her or her family all that well.

Cindy came and stayed in the extra bedroom while my brother and I stayed in our own room. My dad left early on Saturday morning to go to his part-time job. My brother got up about the same time that the young lady woke up. Once I woke up and got dressed, we all had breakfast together. Afterward, my mom said, "I'm going to the grocery store."

I asked, "Are you taking her?"

"No, y'all have fun," she replied.

My mom didn't know that I was sexually active because I'd never let on to that. I was mischievous, but less overt than my little brother, who always did anything I told him to do. "You need to go outside and you need to stay outside until I come and get you," I told my brother.

He said, "Okay."

I ended up in the extra bedroom with our house guest. It took a long time for me to realize that the clock was ticking for my mother's arrival. I was having fun and lost track of time. My brother was still outside, unaware of what was happening in the house. I knew my father was not slated to arrive anytime soon, so I just focused on the two people left at home: me and the young lady.

I didn't even hear the door outside open, declaring my mother's return. Before entering the house, though, she saw Alfred and asked, "Where's your brother?"

"In the house," he said.

"But Cindy's in the house."

"I know," he replied without implication.

So, she opened the bedroom door and witnessed me in a compromised position. She didn't say much at that point. "Y'all need to get up and separate," she said in a tempered tone.

I was very embarrassed, to say the least. One, for being caught, and two, for her revelation about me. Once my father got home, he and my mother had a conversation. I think my mother then drove Cindy to her aunt's house. My dad asked me to come and sit under a tree in our yard and talk to him. We had a conversation that I would never forget.

He said, "Walter Thomas." He never called me by both names unless something was really wrong.

I said, "Yes, sir?"

"Do you know about the birds and bees? Do you know what a rubber is?"

"Yes, sir."

"Do you know how to use it?"

I said, "Yes."

"Have you been using one."

"No."

He said adamantly, "Don't bring a baby in this house."

"No, sir," I responded with assurance.

"Just make sure."

"Okay, Daddy."

That was it for our father-son talk about sex. I knew what he expected, and that was it for me. My father neither gave me a condom, or "rubber," as we called them, nor did he offer to take me to the store to get one. Meanwhile, I had been carrying one in my wallet since middle school, because all the boys did to show off their sexual prowess (even though it was nonexistent in most cases). When I was in high school, the boys would actually buy rubbers and put them in their wallet. Thus, the wallet would serve two main purposes: you would have your high school ID or driver's license, and it was also a place to put your rubber. We had been told in elementary school that we needed to use a rubber whenever we had sex, so every boy that I knew had a rubber in his wallet. I never ever actually used a rubber in high school, and when I finally did later on, I had to get a new one because the one in my wallet had gotten old and mangled.

Alfred did eventually discover what happened that day with Cindy, and that was the last time I tried to send him away while I got into anything of which my parents would disapprove in the house. I don't know how my father broached the subject of sex with him, but I figured that day would be a reference point for Alfred and my dad. For my mother's part, I don't think she was in denial of what I had been doing, for I was a teenager, and teenagers are many times sexually active. Still, the conversation with her about me having sex never came up again. As for Cindy, I would see her at church on occasion when she attended with her aunt, as her mother never came as a member or guest. She was definitely cute, but I wasn't seeking a relationship of any kind. She did seem to have feelings for me.

As a church, even to this day, very little discussion ensues about sex and relationships. It's a taboo subject. When my dad's church invited me to be the Tuesday night Bible study teacher, one of the scriptures that was part of the lexicon of lessons took us to the subject of sex. That night was well attended, more than usual, because everybody wanted to see what I had to say about it. My dad's church knows that I'm very transparent. We were in the book of First Corinthians, chapter seven, which spends a lot of time talking about husband and wife relationships. I think I went on longer that night than I've gone before or since. People were so encouraged by the fact that I had the audacity to broach such a foreign subject because it was off limits for them. When the girls in that church, even now, want to get married, they have no idea of premarital counseling or anything like that related to having a healthy relationship, including sex. In fact, there's no dating before you get married in the Pentecostal Church. The preferred mode is spiritual revelation. If you recognize someone you may be interested in or attracted to, you must go to God to get your answer about whether this person is for you. Meanwhile, you're hoping that simultaneously the other person is talking to God for an answer or direction about you. If God confirms the union in both parties, then the couple can come together in marriage. The next step is going to talk to the pastor about arranging a ceremony. Prior to that, though, there's no hugging, kissing, or intimacy of any kind. There was not even conversation, and such was my life.

13

PIANO HANDS

My mother always taught me to protect my hands because I played the piano. I respected her wishes, but I still wanted to work. I got my first job at the age of 13. I helped Brother Jackson cut yards on weekends and some days during the summer, along with my godbrother Rudolph. He paid us about $7 a day. It was hard work. The mowers had to be pushed and pulled, the hedges were cut with clippers, and we used hoes to clean out the beds, and rakes to take up the leaves and clippings. It was hard work, and it was usually very hot outside. We never saw the inside of any of the houses where we cut yards. We never even met the homeowners. After we finished a landscaping job, we would get in the truck and go home. Jackson would meet the owners to get paid and then he would pay his helpers, like me. That job did not last more than a year. It was too hard and hot.

I liked earning my own money and felt it was part of being a man. My idea of manhood was identified early on by what an older boy or man had in his back pocket. I started carrying a "billfold" wallet just before high school, and I had pictures in it, and my school patrol ID, which I thought was a very big deal. My daddy carried a billfold and he always had large bills in it. He would show me sometimes so I knew how important it was to work and have your own money. This was well before credit cards, so a man was valued by how much he had in his billfold. This was also before crime became so pervasive.

In high school, it became popular for boys not only to carry pictures of girls and close friends in their wallet, but also a "rubber," which was our euphemism for condoms. The rubber was placed inside the bill portion of wallet and over time, the circular shape would be easily identifiable when one took out their wallet. That was supposed to mean that the boy had reached manhood and was having sex. Most of the boys admitted they carried a rubber in their back pocket. I chose rather to carry a small New Testament with the Psalms and Proverbs, and even though I didn't read it often (because the letters were just too small), I wanted to be identified as a church-going boy. Other boys whom my parents called "bad" carried pocketknives, and one or two guys came to school with brass-knuckles to show off.

Life at North Dade Junior Senior High School was heavenly. The students came to North Dade from Rainbow Park and Bunche Park, and we were competitive. I think it was intentional on the part of the teachers to have us believe that the schools were producing the smartest kids. I was placed with several others in my grade in a special homeroom, and we were told at some point we had high stanines, and our progress through high school was being monitored. We were told of other students who were older than we who did well individually, like Eadron Andrews, and Abigail Thompkins, but this was the first time a group of students had been identified as exceptional and bright. In my homeroom were students like Carolyn Eliard, Elva Evans, Brenda Perkins, LaChanze Harrison, Precilla McKenzie, Bridene Grant. The boys in my class were smart too, including Eugene Summerset, Clyde Murphy, and Anthony Taylor. I began to shine more in high school than I had in elementary and middle school.

My mother prayed with me every day before I went to school, and as I got older, she made me pray aloud and she listened, as well as the Lord. She really wanted me to be a good boy, and she would hurt anyone who tried to stop her boys from being "good."

I did my work and played music, but I was not a good athlete. I had only played street football, and not very well until all the better players got tired, and I would stay out there and catch a few passes from John "Fat" Cross. I was never chosen to be on anyone's team until it got down to the last ones and most of the time, I would come in after someone else dropped out or was too tired to play.

Even in PE (Physical Education), I never could climb the rope or run as fast on the 600-yard dash as the others. I was tall, lanky, and slow. My mother did not want me playing tough sports because I would hurt my fingers, and I wouldn't be able to play the piano. So, I concentrated on my music, reading, and academics. I tried to memorize everything I read and apply everything I learned.

In eighth grade, I met this group of boys who lived where we called "across the tracks" in Opa-locka. They were members of the Brownlee family and represented some of the bad boys of that era. A lot of those kids and even their grandkids are either dead or in prison. They just couldn't escape the generational cycle of poverty-driven lawlessness and hopelessness. We had some bad kids who went to school with me who were in gangs. Once I found out about local school gangs, I thought they were the coolest thing. As a matter of fact, I decided I wanted to be a part of something like that. I really did. I thought that I really was cool, and I liked the fact they wore special clothes, such as jeans and banlon shirts. Some of them carried knives or switch blades. The guys who carried switch blades knew how to use them, and they were considered the toughest. Most of the guys just carried a pocketknife for protection or simply to conform. I even had a little one. As I got older, in high school, the kids started carrying weapons because the gangs were pretty bad at my school towards the end of my time there. By the mid '60s, some of the guys came to school with their 22's. My focus remined on music, though.

My favorite teacher at North Dade taught me English and Spanish. Her name was Wallis Hamm Riley, but her last name is Tinnie now. She was very pretty and articulate, armed with high intelligence and poise. She was an incredibly effective teacher, especially given our limited resources in comparison to predominately white neighborhoods. All the students, both male and female, looked forward to going to her class because we knew whenever the semester was over, we would be much better students as a result. Her influence over her students was imposed beyond just the curriculum, for we admired her as a person and professional.

She was good at what she did, and she took her job seriously. When we went to class, she'd be standing by the front door of her classroom awaiting our arrival. She greeted us with a smile as we filed in the room, and she was always eager to ger her lesson started. It was as if she was just as anxious to teach us every day, and she maintained that demeanor for the whole time we were in school. For 7th, 8th, and 9th grade, we had other good English teachers, such as Annie McRae and Carolyn Young.

However, when we got to 10th grade, Ms. Riley took it to another level. She elevated our knowledge and appreciation of great literature like no one else ever had.

Ms. Riley worked almost exclusively with accelerated students. Because of elevated standardized test scores, a group of us were identified as having "high stanines," and were being pushed to take more challenging coursework with teachers like Ms. Riley. We were somewhat marked for success and often took our classes together.

Somehow, I felt that Ms. Riley sensed our potential and was dedicated to pushing us. We later found out that she, herself, was always a go-getter. Brilliant, she apparently excelled in college, working on the newspaper staff along with another one of our teachers. When she came to North Dade in about 1958, she was fresh out of college and wanted to make her mark. She brought out the best in her students and had us reading literature that other black kids weren't reading in our high school (and probably others). We read books by Chaucer and Homer's "The Iliad" and "The Odyssey." She was fluent in Spanish and could hold an entire conversation with her students in Spanish, which she would require at times. We had no white or Hispanic teachers at our school, so the black teachers taught Spanish and other language classes.

Eventually, I did have one white teacher, Jean Laughlin. She taught music for one year as a substitute for Mr. Jones, who moved to Ponce de Leon Middle School. She was a nice person, but she was a terrible music teacher. The school had apparently brought her in to teach music and lead the choir. Because Miss Laughlin was so ineffective, I ended up doing most of the teaching during my 11th grade year. She didn't play well. She didn't sing well. She didn't know black music. She was just a fill-in for us, but I had to fill in for her. She lasted one year and had no impact on me, but I'm sure I impacted her, because she didn't know what to do. She was lost, out of her culture, but she did the best she could. I was the student choral director, so I arranged and practiced with members of the boys' and girls' choral ensemble. Highly skilled at the piano, playing from sheet music and by ear, I became central to music production both at church and school.

I thought one day I may become a music teacher, but I had never imagined becoming a professional musician who actually got paid for just playing. I had seen other popular music teachers who had graduated from college, and I wanted to be like them. I knew that I could take my training and go to college to play in the band and then later use it at the church, but I didn't see myself as a church musician. When I was growing up in church, there weren't many professional church musicians. It was something you did for your church. You weren't paid necessarily. I never got a penny for playing at my church. I did, however, get paid for playing for other churches. For example, we had a classmate that drowned when I was in the 10th grade, and they asked the school junior choir to sing at the funeral at Mount Hermon AME Church. My music teacher was the organist for that funeral service, and I played the piano. We performed "The Lord is My Shepherd," which was a very popular choir song at the time, but it was also very difficult to play. The pastor, whose name was Sam Gaye, approached my music teacher and said, "Who's that guy, the young man playing the piano?"

He said, "That's my student. Don't you need a piano player, someone that can play?" They had someone who could clunk on the keys, but no one who could play well. The pastor hired me, and that was my first job as a musician where I got paid. I think I made $10 or $15 every time I played at a service. It wasn't much, but it was more than I had ever earned.

14

HOMECOMING

Family reunions were regular occurrences, so we traveled as a family every summer to North Carolina by car or by train. We drove most of the time, because Daddy wanted to ensure that he had a way of getting around town. He never wanted to beg anyone to give him "a lift" to go anywhere while in North Carolina. Our vacations almost always started with the Richardsons in Anson County.

For years, the Richardsons had been gathering annually in Ansonville, N.C., but then moved the gathering to Wadesboro, N.C., for what is now called our "family reunion." During this time, on Sept. 10, 1962, at age 79, my grandfather Frank J. Richardson died in Wadesboro. In 1962, and years prior to this, however, the event was called "homecoming." Homecoming always took place on the fourth Sunday in August so that the family from all over North Carolina could gather to attend church, pray together, introduce the newest arrivals to the clan, and celebrate the life of the oldest members of the family.

Locally, the Richardsons were regarded as the offspring of my great grandfather, Reverend Frank Richardson, who founded Pleasant Hill Baptist Church in 1870. As his children became adults and moved to other parts of the state and country, the tradition was adopted for everyone to gather each year back at our central home location: the church. Pleasant Hill Baptist Church was built on property owned by Frank Richardson and was a small wood-frame structure with an accompanying cemetery. The plans were for all Richardsons to be funeralized and buried in the family plot. My grandfather, Frank J. Richardson, had 10 children, and all of them were raised attending Pleasant Hill Baptist Church. All Rev. Frank Richardson's brothers and sisters attended Pleasant Hill, and the grandchildren, which included my father, were also raised in the family church. Obviously, as the children became grown or married and lived in the area, they remained as part of the Pleasant Hill church family. My grandfather Frank was a deacon there along with my great-uncle "Uncle Fet" McClendon.

Every year, dozens of the members of Pleasant Hill Church would come to Ansonville, dressed in their finest to attend the services at 11a.m. on the 4th Sunday in August. The most memorable part of the worship was the congregational singing which was always led by the men. Deacon Charlie Little was famous for leading the singing. He was animated, with his right hand covering his right ear, with eyes closed singing those Carolina airs. Carolina airs consisted of choruses where the leader sang the melody line, and other members of the congregation would join in and sing a harmony line just above the melody line.

The most forgettable part of the worship experience was the preaching. The preacher, of whom I can't remember any, would always come in late, dressed in a dull black robe, almost unaware that people were singing, and literally would not move until time to preach. The windows would be closed in the unair-conditioned church, and the doors closed until he finished his sermon. People would be fanning, humming, sweating, and waiting for his sermon to end.

Following services, the women would hastily get to their cars to open their trunks where food prepared for everyone to taste had been stored. Everyone wanted to have some of everyone else's delicacies. While the ladies prepared on card tables, makeshift tables, and tree stumps, children and men would wander around the premises to look at graves and grave markers, walking through the crusty red clay of the Carolinas.

This church event would last from 11a.m. until around 2 p.m., at which time the primary Richardson clan, my grandmother's family, the Masks, and the descendants of Frank and Ollie would gather for dessert and fresh fruit, usually watermelon. The atmosphere was always joyous, the children wild, the flies plentiful, the weather hot, and the stories fascinating.

We arrived on Friday, August 23, for the 1963 homecoming. My mother spent the night, but Saturday she spent the day in Albemarle where her relatives lived, and where she had been brought up. My mother did not particularly care for the Richardson side of the family. She had been treated strangely by some of them, largely because she was very dark-skinned. The Richardson's were considered by many, and they considered themselves, just a little better than others. All of Frank and Ollie's children graduated from high school and attended either college or trade schools. Other families in that area did not have that story. Most of the children were fair-complexioned, tall, and athletically built. All the girls played basketball in high school, and some in college. All the boys were athletes in high school, and Dad and my Uncle Amos played semi-pro basketball during the summers to make extra money. So other families that were not of the same socioeconomic and physical status of the Richardsons were not considered peers.

Mother came back on Sunday afternoon following the homecoming service so my daddy could prepare to leave that Monday for the March on Washington planned for Wednesday, August 28. My Aunt Helen was a schoolteacher in Baltimore, and we would be spending time with her and friends. Our plans were to leave from Baltimore and drive back to Miami. Aunt Helen was taking my cousins Elaine and Edward Lee Bennett to Baltimore, too, so we would all be together for the March and other activities we would enjoy while in the area. I wanted to wear my favorite outfit for the March: my blue seersucker pants, my new red banlon shirt, and matching socks.

When we arrived, my brother and I and my parents met the girl who lived next door to my Aunt Hattie Diggs in Baltimore. Her name was Mona Lisa. She was the same age, and we were just about the same height. I was already six feet tall by then, and this girl could look me in my eyes. She had light skin and was mesmerizing to me. She talked plenty but didn't have the best diction. Instead of her saying "cover," she would say "cuber." She would say "cooch" instead of "couch."

Her mother allowed her to hang out with me, and we ended up going to a couple of events together. At my request and her own interest, she accompanied us to the March. She sat in the middle, between me and my brother, on our first stop to visit the Tomb of the Unknowns. This is a monument dedicated to military personnel who died without their remains being identified. The military guard at the monument is changed in an elaborate ceremony, which is called the Changing of the Guard, which happens every hour (or every half hour, depending on the time of year). This was certainly exciting and memorable, but it couldn't compete with

Mona Lisa. The next day, we went to the March on Washington, and she was with me the whole time. The crowd was thick and the environment electric, but I didn't hear a thing that Dr. Martin Luther King, Jr., said that day. I didn't hear what John Lewis was saying. I only heard Mahalia Jackson singing, because I had my eyes glued on Mona Lisa. My intention was that she remained fixated on me, as I wore blue seersucker pants with a red banlon shirt and socks swathed in black Flagg Brother shoes. When we went home to Miami, she and I stayed in contact until the 10th grade or so. By my junior year, I started liking somebody else who lived in town. The long-distance thing wasn't working for me.

15

BURGEONING ATHLETE, MUSICIAN AND SPEAKER

At the invitation of my art teacher, Leroy Daniels, I did eventually try out for the track team. He thought with my being tall and lanky, there might be an event that I could, over time, excel in. I remember the first day of practice in the 8th grade running around the large field. It was not a track field, but a large lot purchased by the school board for us to utilize for special events. The baseball team practiced at the far end of the gated lot, and the track team, at least during track season, had the use of the area closest to the classrooms. Cones had been set up to mark the oval area that was our quarter-mile running area. Mr. Daniels and some assistants had marked the area off using a long tape measure.

The boys ran slowly around the field, over and over again, while the coach just watched. He told us we would have practice every day after school. After about a week of running around the field and doing exercises, including jumping jacks, sit-ups, and lying on our backs pushing up other team members with our legs, we then began running on the road. About the third week in, we started organizing into events. I already knew I was not a sprinter. Gerald Arline and some of the other boys were just too fast. So, I attempted the quarter mile. There were boys that were much faster than I, but I kept up pretty well. Afterall, I was only in the 8th grade. The half-mile was much too long.

The coach then advised me to try out for the high jump. We only had one boy jumping, so I tried that, and at our first track meet against another team, I was the team's second-best high jumper. I was already about 6' and the goal was for me to jump my height, eventually. I think I cleared 5 feet at our first meet, or 5 feet 2 inches at the most. But that got me a third place in our dual school meet. That was the best I could do that meet. Towards the end of the track season, Mr. Daniels, whom we affectionately called "Uncle Dan," started me on the hurdles. We didn't have any hurdlers at our school, so this would be an event where I could prove to be the best, at least at North Dade.

The librarian, Mrs. Wilson, ordered a filmstrip for me to watch that showed the techniques athletes who ran the hurdles used. I started watching with more intensity than the boys who ran hurdles from the other schools; most were not that good, except Harvey Nairn from Northwestern High School. He had speed and form. So, in the 8th grade, even after track season, I studied running the hurdles.

As a 10th grader, I placed 5th in the district for the high hurdles. Harvey Nairn won the state meet that year with a time of 14.4, which was considered fast in 1964. The next year, I came in second in the state meet in the high hurdles. In 1966, my senior year, I was undefeated and won the local, district and state meet in the high hurdles, breaking Harvey Nairn's record. My record would stand forever, since the state decided that year would be the last year of all-black high school competition. From that time forward all high schools were parts of the same athletic conference, divided only by school size and region. I also won the low hurdles at the state competition and ran the second leg on the mile-relay team that came in second place.

I also excelled in music in high school, joining the junior chorus and playing piano for all the choirs, assembly programs, and other events in the 7th grade. Mr. Charles Jones became my piano teacher, taking over from Mrs. Dunn, who lived too far for my family to drive me for lessons. He lived not far from our house and was an excellent instructor, even though he liked to touch and tap on me while I practiced with him. For some reason, my mother never let me go to his house alone, despite the fact that Mr. Jones had another man that was "rooming" with him. She always sat with us in the living room while I was taking lessons.

Mr. Jones later purchased an Allen Organ and began teaching me how to play that instrument, since it was suspected that I would be a church musician at some point. He did manage to get me away from my mother once to take a lesson on the three-manual organ at The Church of the

Transfiguration. Playing in that sanctuary took my breath away. The organ had real pipes.

I learned to speak well publicly with the training I received both in church and in high school. English was my favorite subject, and I learned to articulate well. Mrs. Betty Smiley, Mrs. Carolyn Young, and Mrs. Wallis Hamm Riley were excellent speakers, and I ended up, along with Elva Evans, Gloria Parker, Sharon Hudson, LaChanze Harrison, and Carolyn Eliard, getting a few speaking opportunities. So I joined the Thespian Club and was, with my speaking and singing ability, involved in drama under the tutelage of Mr. James Randolph. Because of my ability to debate and speak, I ended up being, I think, the homeroom president, then class president of the junior year and senior year classes. I was also salutatorian, which came as a complete surprise to me, ranking second highest in my graduating class of 1966. I thought Clyde Murphy would get that award, and apparently he did too. I remember hearing that his mother, who taught Home Economics at North Dade, checked diligently with the office staff to ascertain if the grade averages of our graduating class were correct.

Carolyn Eliard and I received notice at the end of our 11th grade year that we were eligible for an "early admission" scholarship to attend Talledega College, but both our parents declined that opportunity. During our senior year, several of us were selected to participate in a dual enrollment program sponsored by Miami Dade Junior College, and then we were given a chance to take courses over the summer after graduation. My homeroom classmate Barry Shellman and I rode to school together that summer. He had been accepted to Bethune-Cookman College on a scholarship, and I had narrowed my choices to Florida A&M and Fisk University, because both schools had offered me scholarships in music. After our classes at Miami Dade ended, we all knew we would soon go our separate ways.

I was class president in 12th grade and had been student body president since I was in the 7th grade. I was a popular, well-respected student, largely because my daddy was a well-respected preacher in the community. Our family was known for its integrity and community support. Most saw me a as "good boy" with lots of great character, talent, and promise. I was often tagged with another admirable student named Clyde Murphy, who ended up going to Yale and becoming the lawyer who became the director of the NAACP National Defense and Educational Fund. He and I were among the 138 students who comprised the graduating class of 1966, and I was salutatorian.

16

R A T T L E D

I didn't leave for college on time because my parents and I still could not decide where I was going to attend school. I had two separate scholarships offers. One from FAMU for track and music, and I had one scholarship to Fisk for music. Although those two schools were my main focus, I also had other scholarship offers for track. In high school, the coaches wanted me to prepare for the '68 Olympics.

I received a call from Fisk University inquiring whether I was going to attend because I had already received my room assignment and everything was ready for me. They wanted me to be a part of the Fisk Jubilee singers, which was set up for me by my high school music teacher, Marsha McIver. I then advised them, in my mother's presence, that I had no intention of traveling to Tennessee. So, my attention turned to FAMU in Tallahassee, Florida.

The woman in charge of the FAMU Concert Chorale, Rebecca Steele, had come down from Tallahassee and interviewed several of us to be a part of her music program. She was apparently impressed with my interview and the audition I'd done with her colleague, Mary Roberts. She offered me and several other students a music scholarship, which I decided to take. I was excited because I was going to play for and sing with the FAMU Chorale.

With my father's assistance, I got a summer job at Sears before leaving for college. I was one of the first black salespeople in the clothing department. There was a black man named Danny Evans who sold paint, and there was another black person who had just gotten promoted and was selling tires. I sold men's clothing at our location. At the same time, my father retired from

Sears. He had been pastoring the church since his Aunt Mamie's death the previous year in May 1965, and the responsibility of managing both the church and work got to be too much.

As a high school senior, I was already attending classes at Miami Dade Community College as a dual-enrollment student, and I decided to take advantage of the opportunity to earn some college credits over the summer. So, I was working and taking classes, and as a result, I missed one of the most significant opportunities for any music-minded student at FAMU: playing in the renowned marching band, "The Marching 100." People who wanted to be in the band had to go early for tryouts. Some of my classmates did, and they were able to join the band.

When I didn't show up on time there, my high school friend and fellow high school band member Eugene Smith called me to find out where I was. I told him I was "on my way." My parents got my things together and asked our family friend Anthony Turner, who taught Drivers' Education at Northwestern, to take me to college. He agreed.

I registered for classes late, but I immediately wanted to find out how I could still get in the "Marching 100." Rehearsals had already started, and the freshman class selection had passed. Nevertheless, I was allowed to audition, but was told that I couldn't participate until the following year. Mrs. Steele found out, I think from Dr. Foster, that I was trying out for the band even though I was on a Choral Music scholarship, and my time on the "patch" ended. Even though I was good enough, I never marched onto the football field with the band. I played a few times at the Savoy, a local night club, and spent some time in French town, where blacks lived and socialized.

Meanwhile, my father was having issues with the church back home, and he needed my support. He had been serving for just over a year as the pastor, and his transition from working at Sears to being a spiritual leader was not smooth. One day, I got an emergency phone call from my dad. After I got back to my dorm room, I noticed a note that one of my classmates had put on my door. It said to "call home as soon as possible." So, I went down the hall to where the phone was and called home. Apparently, there was a faction of the membership that was following him, but there was a larger faction that was allying themselves with another guy who thought he should have been selected as the pastor. They actually ended up going to court. My dad trusted absolutely no one, so this was an extremely difficult period for him. This was the first time the church had ever been embroiled in any kind of controversial situation about anything.

My dad told me, "I don't care how you get here or when you get here, but I need you to leave and come home as soon as you can." Given his appeal, I left FAMU about a day later and returned home to assist my dad. Daddy suggested I go back to FAMU after the holidays to continue once I helped him with a few details on pastoring and leading. I could tell that he really wanted me to stay home, but he knew I needed my college education.

I decided to remain in Miami to support my father, so I got my job back at Sears in the men's department as a salesman. Since my father had worked at that store for over 20 years, he had some influence with the personnel department. I loved my job, but I dodged people who knew me from high school and knew I was supposed to be away at college. I subsequently enrolled again at Miami-Dade Junior College. I was not as good a student at Miami-Dade as I was in high school. Instead of making all A's, I was making B's and C's. I had to study hard. The concepts were new, the environment strange, and the students and faculty were not social, at least the kind of social I was used to in high school and college where almost everyone was black. At Miami-Dade, almost everyone was white. I didn't understand them, their customs, their attitudes, their dress, their jokes, and their reasoning. And they didn't understand much about me. Plus, I was working a full-time job and helping my father at the church, so I made no real effort to transcend our apparent differences.

Earlier in 1966, just prior to attending college, I had a tremendous spiritual experience during a revival. I got saved. I had been attending church all my life, but I never got saved, dedicating my life to the Lord. By the end of the revival, many of the saints' children and church youth received salvation and were baptized during one of the church's largest baptismal services. The baptismal pool was located in the front yard of the church and resembled a grave with a wooden A-shaped cover.

I played for the worship services on piano and guitar, and I began organizing a church choir. I took the knowledge I had from high school, the exposure (though limited) I had from FAMU, and the natural gifts given me by the Master, and I organized an adult choir. In one year, I taught them to sing in three-part harmony. That style of singing had to be taught because singing in the Pentecostal church was most often random or Spirit-led. Several church and community choirs had begun to make gospel music more popular, and we learned many of the songs of that era.

Our church had never had a choir before, so I began the church choir under some kind of strange understanding about who would be in charge. Because I was a "young" Christian, they couldn't name me as "director," so I was named a musician. Even though I was in charge of everything, and I taught everything, my mother was called director because she was a seasoned Christian. My mother and a lady named Sister Maxine Edwards were officially in charge, but I was really the choir director.

We sang a lot of traditional choir music, but we also did what was current and contemporary. I also wrote some of the music, so our choir was always cutting-edge. Church attendance started growing because of the integration of new music. Because it was a Pentecostal church and the requirements were strict to be a member, membership didn't grow—just attendance did. A lot of people came to the church, particularly on Sunday night, when the choir was being featured. People drove from Richmond Heights, Hollywood, and Fort Lauderdale to hear the choir sing.

17

GOAT'S MILK REVELATION

Dolores and I both got saved in 1966 before I went away to college. She got saved in May, and I got saved in July, a month after high school graduation. A couple dozen of us high school seniors and juniors got saved at the same time, which was a rarity. Typically, people came to the Lord singularly or in pairs, not groups, as the lifestyle standards in the church were pretty high. You couldn't drink or smoke. No premarital sex was allowed, and ladies couldn't wear pants. I didn't see my first movie until 1963, when I was in 10th grade. The first movie I saw happened to be by The Beatles called a "Hard Day's Night." Ironically, it was something musical.

At that time, Pentecostal churches didn't allow voting or involvement in politics of any kind, at any level. We didn't salute the flag. We didn't serve in the military. They rejected politics based on Christ's statements about His kingdom not belonging to this world, so they focused on His spiritual realm and not earthly politics. Our church was like that until my father took over. The NAACP kind of pressed upon us the fact that we were citizens of both domains. My family was very involved in civil rights, so at age 15, I already had my NAACP card. Being socially conscious or civic-minded was a requirement in my family.

Because our social relationships were confined to church, I didn't really see myself dating anyone seriously outside our church. Dolores was probably the best-looking young lady at the church. She was older than I, but I think that made her even more appealing. Given all these constraints, I felt like the only person who would understand me as a person and could tolerate my growth as a Christian without being confining was Dolores. To me, there were no other potential options at the church. My mother, meanwhile, had somebody else in mind for me, and she kept pushing that young lady in my face at church. She was tall, but she had no other salient features. Dolores had already gone to Hampton University in Virginia, but we corresponded weekly while she was away, not as boyfriend-girlfriend, just as friends. We became pen pals. We came from the same religious background, and we had the same values. Thus, corresponding with her was stress-free.

She left college because the lifestyle was just too much, given the fact that she came from a strict religious background. Too much was going on there that was opposed to her faith. She felt it best that she leave that environment. As a result, she moved to California with relatives and stayed there because she had a job with the post office. She didn't stay there long before moving back to Miami with her family. So, the year that I finished high school was about the same year that she came home and started working.

Before I went to FAMU, I told my girlfriend, Patricia Williams, that we could no longer date because I just got saved and I was getting ready to go to college. I didn't think about dating anyone else seriously until I left school and met another young lady from North Carolina in the summer of 1967. She was gorgeous, intelligent, and spiritual. I even found the fact that she was short, at about 5 feet 4 inches, endearing. My former girlfriend Pat was 5 feet 10 inches, and I was typically attracted to taller women. Everything about this girl intrigued me, though. She went back to college in North Carolina in the fall, and we kept in touch for a while. Our communication tapered off and my focus returned to Dolores, who was suffering from stomach ulcers. I was available to help her because she was also working at Sears at that time. I was able to take her to get her goat's milk, which was recommended as a remedy for her ailment.

The goat's milk farm was down near the Tamiami Trail. She lived in Liberty City, and I lived further north in Opa-locka, but I would still pick her up to get the goat milk. It was as if I was helping family, because we have been close all our lives. I've known her since I was born. In fact, on the day I was dedicated, all the church members were outside, and my daddy was sitting down holding me. A little girl was standing to the side of my dad. That little girl happened to be Dolores.

She and I got a little closer during the time we worked together. Not long after helping her through her medical condition, I decided that perhaps she should be the person that I would spend the rest of my life with. We talked about that, and she agreed. I knew all of her boyfriends, and she knew all of my girlfriends because we had no secrets. We're both very strong Christians coming from two very strong Christian families, and that weighed heavily on my decision to marry her. As things got a little heavier between us and we both agreed that God had indeed chosen her to be my wife, things moved rather quickly. We knew marriage was imminent.

Dolores had never been involved in an intimate romantic relationship before we wed on December 7, 1968, and I think we may have kissed twice prior to that day. We moved right after our wedding to a home I had purchased with my dad's assistance. It was not far from his house, just two blocks, on the same street. This house had four bedrooms and one bathroom, which was larger than my dad's home with three bedrooms and one bathroom, though both were built by the same developer. The house cost $64,000, and my payments were $68 per month because I put down a huge down payment. In anticipation of my marriage, I also purchased a 1968 Chevrolet Impala. I wanted the best accommodations for my new bride. We both had good, stable jobs, the best we could get for two reasonably intelligent young people. We had both attended college, but neither of us had undergraduate degrees at that time. So, I worked at Sears as a division manager, giving me responsibility for scheduling employees' work hours, ordering, displaying, and returning merchandise, and handling customers' complaints. Dolores worked at Jackson Memorial Hospital in the accounting department. We both paid our tithes to the church, saved about ten percent from every paycheck, and lived well within our means. We both liked to dress well, so when we purchased clothes, we spent just a little more so we could buy better outfits or the best clothes we could afford. Good was never what we desired for each other.

We were young, and perhaps too young, in some people's opinion, to be married. However, we were among the norm at our church in terms of young couples, as there were several people in the church just slightly older than we or the same age as we were when we got married. My godbrother, Thomas Phillip Edwards, got married at age 20, and his wife Maxine was 18. She had just graduated from Dorsey High School. After she got saved, she knew the requirements for marriage. She wasn't going to go away to college because that was almost frowned upon at my church; the teaching was that adult members would obtain a local job, typically a service job, so they could remain affiliated with the church to become a disciple. The church felt that members who went to college would be impressed with "man's knowledge," which could conflict with the knowledge of God. I was steeped in the tradition of my faith, but I still knew my life and ministry had a slightly different calling, one that would take me out in the world and not be secluded from it.

By 1968, I had also started preaching on street corners after Sunday services as an evangelist. I figured this was a way to get people's attention, at least until I got through initially sharing my testimony and could add a verse of scripture then add a short devotional. I'm not sure how many folks I impacted, but I know my method of sharing made the preparation for street meetings simpler. Once I started preaching in the building, behind the pulpit, I started explaining short verses of scripture by using a rhyming method. My points of emphasis would be memorable if I cued the listeners with poetic words. For example, I preached once about Jesus feeding the multitudes, and spoke of the "little lost lad who loaned the Lord his lunch!" That went over big at Tabernacle, and that style of presenting soon became my mainstay.

In the Key of M

18

LIKE FATHER, LIKE SON

When I got ready to go off to college, a friend said to me, "What are you gonna major in when you go to college? You'll probably be a preacher, like your dad."

"Hell no," I replied adamantly. I never wanted to be a preacher like my father. I saw my path as bigger, more diverse, and something that included music professionally. To my surprise, though, I ended up not only becoming a preacher, but also yielding a great amount of my time to supporting church members and community causes, just like my father had. Among the means of support, my father would appear in court for church members' kids who had gotten in trouble with the law, go car shopping with people so they didn't get ripped off with the financing, and visit sick people in the hospital or at home to offer prayer and words of support. During the genocide in Rwanda in 1994, when "children were being left homeless and without parents," my father led church members to provide hundreds of dollars' worth of medical supplies and clothing (Tinsley 2017). He said the church paid more than $3,000 just in shipping costs to get the donations to the children there. I watched my father support and give all that he could to others to the point of exhaustion. I thought, *"That's not going to be my life."* That was my sentiment until I had my own family and church. The occurrence of the former, having a family, happened sooner than I thought, and the evolution of the latter, leading a church, was more protracted than others would have thought.

Having gotten married at age 20, I saw a lot of changes occurring in my life, as well as the world at large, particularly in Vietnam. We had not been married long before Uncle Sam called on me in 1969 to serve in the war.

I began serving as a "conscientious objector," assigned by the military to work in the State Nursery Division. By definition, a conscientious objector is someone who is opposed to serving in the armed forces and/or bearing arms on the grounds of moral or religious principles (Conscientious Objectors n.d.). The camp where I worked was responsible for primarily growing pine trees to be used in military and other similar operations as natural protection. These trees were not available to consumers, because they grew upwards of 12 feet per year until they reached their full height of 30-40 feet in just 2-3 years. I remember bringing one home for my dad to plant in his yard, but after about 6 months, Daddy got rid of it. Every weekend, if we were on schedule with planting, weeding, and harvesting trees, and if there were no forest fires to address, I would drive 180 miles from Punta Gorda to Opa-locka.

When Dolores announced that she was pregnant, I was the happiest and most scared person in the world. I was able to watch Dolores' body and mood changes. She often craved strange foods, which I thought was funny. She gained quite a bit of weight and began to look quite different from the slim-but-tall 115-pound lady I married. Then one weekend, I got word that Dolores was experiencing labor pains. She was taken to the Mt. Sinai Hospital on Miami Beach, where my son was born on January 10, 1971. I was overjoyed about the miracle of his presence and his health. He had all of his fingers and toes. I know because I counted them over and over again. My responsibility was to give him his first name. We knew we didn't want a junior, but we couldn't settle on a middle name. Juniors were rare in both our families; except Dolores' brother Abraham was a junior. We named him Walter LaMark Richardson, but we all called him "Mark."

This boy was spoiled. My mother and father spoiled me and my brother with affection, time, and gifts, and so this new addition to the Richardson family would be likewise spoiled with affection, time, and gifts. As soon as Mark was dedicated, Dolores returned to work, and my momma took care of the baby.

I separated from the service on May 18, 1972, a little over a year after Mark was born, and he became the center of my attention. He went everywhere with me so he could see what his daddy was doing. I'd put him in the back seat of my Volkswagen to take him to church. I wanted Mark to play the piano, so I taught him how to play. He was about 8 years old when

I had him play a James Cleveland song that I taught him for a concert at Second Baptist Church. I made him practice the song "Lord, Do It for Me" every day. Cleveland had taught me how to play it, so I was excited about showing that my son had learned it, too. Wanting to leave a musical legacy, I pressured him to practice and play, but he ended up not playing the piano. He did, however, become an excellent saxophonist, and he still plays well now. He got a full ride to go to Jackson State University to be in a band. He could have gone to Florida A&M, but he did not want to be in that band.

A few years ago, I bought a saxophone for me because I play as well. My son came home for Christmas with his family and he sees my horn. He puts my mouthpiece on and starts playing Christmas songs, which his own kids had never heard him play before. In fact, I hadn't heard him play since college.

Three years after the birth of Mark, my daughter, LaKisha, was born on May 12th in Good Samaritan Hospital in West Palm Beach, Florida. Like my father, I now had two kids and was preaching. I treasured my family and wanted to provide them with everything I could. One of those things was, of course, music. Although my daughter could play the piano, her instrument of choice was the violin. She is still involved in music as the assistant director of the church choir.

Like my father, I was always proud of my children and wanted the best for them. I didn't necessarily want them to be just like me or their mother; I wanted them to be even better. With that in mind, I was willing to work hard to provide for my family, so I decided to focus on my career opportunities with Sears.

The burial headsone of Colman and his wife Charlotte

My grandfather Frank Richardson picking cotton in front of his house in Ansonville, N.C., circa 1945

Aunt Marjorie Richardson Robinson's service station in Wadesboro, N.C.

Robinson-Richardson family house in Wadesboro, N.C. circa 1962

The six Richardson sisters, my aunts Annie Rachel, Hattie, Mildred, Mamie Helen, Marjorie and Sadie. All of them played basketball in high school, and at least one of them played basketball in college

93

With my granduncle
Elder Thomas James
Richardson, founder
of The Church of
God Tabernacle
(True Holiness), and
from whom I got my
middle name

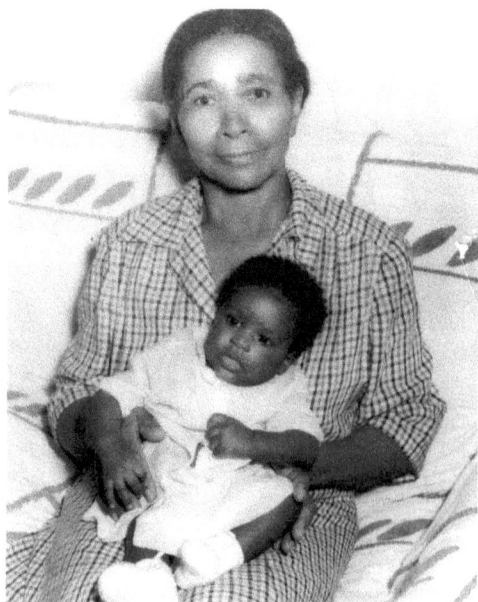

My Grandmother Ollie
Richardson, who came to Miami
from North Carolina to assist my
mother shortly after I was born,
circa 1948

My father Walter H. Richardson (right) with his uncle Elder Thomas James Richardson (left), circa 1948

Walter T. Richardson (right) in front of our house in Miami, circa 1949

Congregation of The Church of God Tabernacle (True Holiness) for my christening, six weeks after my birth, circa 1948. My father is holding me (center) and the little girl to my father's right, who was 3 years old, was my wife, Dolores.

My father, Walter H. Richardson (right of the bride), was the best man at his friend's wedding and attended with my mother, Poseline (to his right). It took place at "The Headquarters." Also pictured is my aunt Mamie Richardson (right of my mother).

My parents and I around 1952. Photo taken by Abraham Turner, Sr. who would end up being my father-in-law

My brother Alfred James Richardson (left), age 2, in front of our home in April 1955 in Liberty City

High school drum major, 1965

High school graduation, North Dade, 1966

Official picture for Sears Roebuck & Co when I was appointed personnel manager at the West Palm Beach store, 1973

Delivering the invocation at the Florida Int'l university's commencement ceremony where Major League Baseball Hall of Famer Joe DiMaggio was awarded an honorary doctorate

Having lunch with Attallah Shabazz, the oldest daughter of civil rights activist Malcolm X and Betty Shabazz

Gladys Knight and I discussing what she would sing at her mother-in-law's funeral. She was then married to motivational speaker Les Brown. I was her accompanist.

Attending the first day of the murder trial of Trayvon Martin. Trayvon's parents, Sabrina Fulton and Tracy Martin, requested my presence. Trayvon's mother, Sabrina, was raised in Opa Locka, FL, where her mother and I lived on the same block

Attorney Ben Crump (rear) and Sabrina Fulton (right) look on as Tracy Martin, Trayvon Martin's father, thanks me for attending the first day of trial for his son's killer in 2013.

My father in ministry, Rev. John A. Ferguson (left), at my retirement party in May 2010 with my father, Bishop Walter H. Richardson

Fellow chaplain for the Miami-Dade Police Department Deacon Tom Hanlon scheduled to provide prayers for a police ceremony, Jan. 28, 2016

My brother, Alfred Richardson (left), my father Walter H. Richardson (center), and I (right)

Four generations of Richardson men (left to right): Walter L. Richardson, Walter H. Richardson, Walter C. Richardson, Walter T. Richardson

President Bill Clinton and I at Janet Reno's funeral at Miami-Dade College South Campus, November 2016

Speaking with my good friend, the late U.S. Attorney General Janet Reno, who was an honorary member of Sweet Home

Honored by President Barack Obama after providing special chaplaincy services to the Secret Service.

My wife and I with South African Anglican bishop and theologian Desmond Mpilo Tutu

Receiving an honorary doctorate degree in 1996 from Saint Thomas University along with the late professional baseball player Tommy Lasorda (center) one year after earning my doctorate degree in pastoral counseling

My father, Walter H. Richardson, with Bishop Jacob Cohen during his consecration service as bishop at The Church of God Tabernacle (True Holiness) in 1995

Commencement Ceremony 2015 at St. Thomas University where I taught for 26 years. Area AME pastor Yaxley Jamison received his MDiv Degree.

Ribbon cutting ceremony for Sweet Home Missionary Baptist Church in January 2009. This was the second sanctuary building erected under my pastorate. Sweet Home's congregation grew from approximately 100 members to a membership of several thousand from 1983–2010.

Bishop Adam J. Richardson and I attending the funeral of our friend Dr. Arthur T. Jones at Bible-Based Fellowship Church in Tampa. We were both musicians and ministers with the same last name, so people often confused us since the 1960s.

Grande Lum (center), former Director of the U.S. Department of Justice's Community Relations Service. I served then as the Chairman of the Miami-Dade Community Relations Board.

The Miami-Dade Community Relations Board in 2017 when I served as chairman. Commissioner Jean Monestine, standing behind me, is the county's first Haitian American member and was commission chairman when this picture was taken.

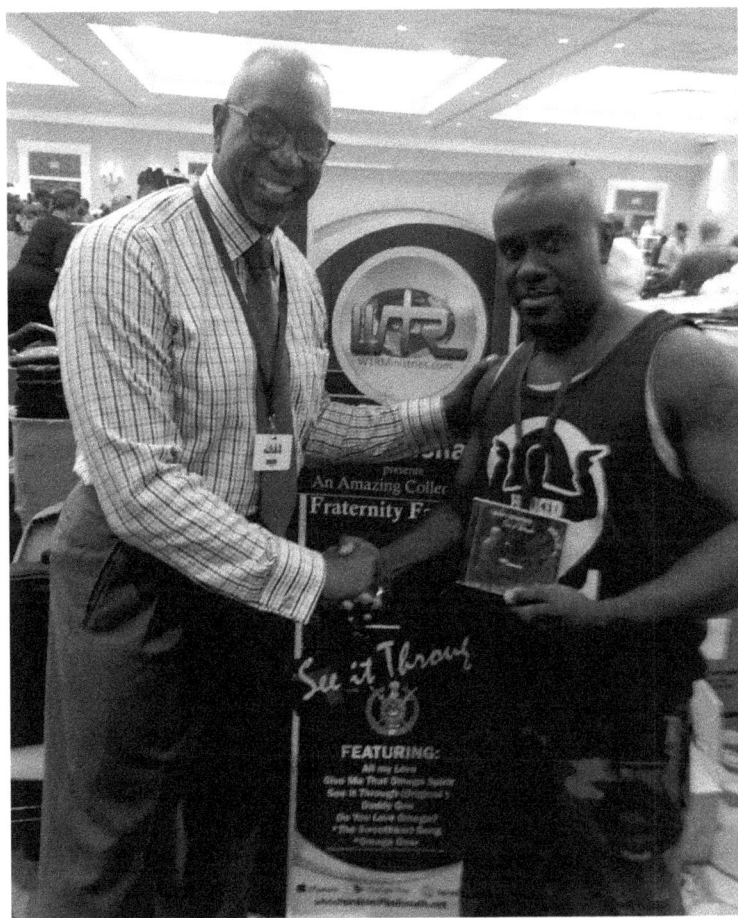

Release of my CD "See it Through" in Las Vegas, Nevada, in 2016

Coach Todd Bowles and I on the field before the December
2015 Jets vs. Patriots football game. I was the Jets' guest
chaplain and they won that game.

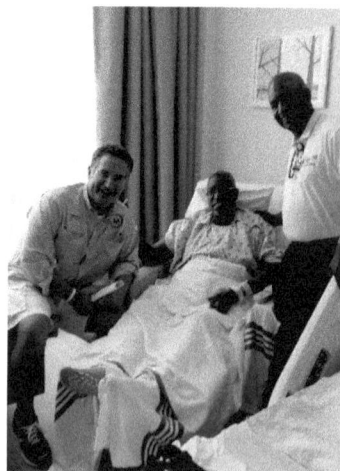

The day after robotic surgery
for prostate cancer in 2013

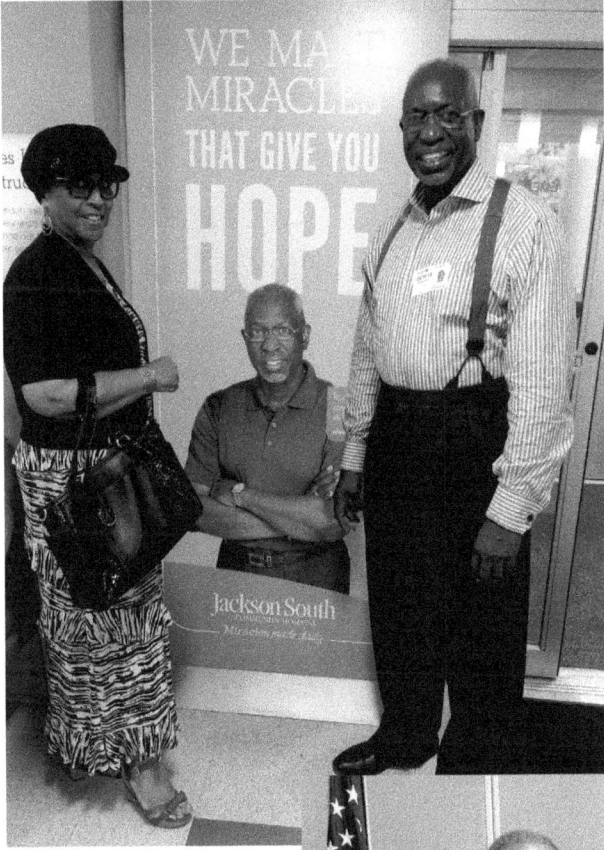

My wife, Dolores, and I standing at the entrance of Jackson South Medical Center's Emergency Room in front of a poster featuring me as a recovered cancer patient.

Former U.S. Attorney General Eric Holder and I following a meeting of community leaders exploring the possibility of him running for president in 2016

Married my wife, Dolores,
on December 7, 1968

My wife and I on our first
cruise

Celebrating one of my many
pastoral anniversaries with my
wife, Dolores

My wife and our kids: daughter LaKisha and son Walter L. Richardson at an MCCJ dinner honoring my interfaith work in the community

With my wife and our kids, daughter LaKisha and son Walter L. Richardson at Sweet Home anniversary

19

SEARS SERVICE OF INCLUSION

My mother had always told me that, in order to advance in a world that would try to exclude me, I was going to have to do better than my counterparts. She emphasized this in my every expression: dress, music, speech, and writing. I was on a newspaper staff, so writing came almost naturally to me. When I came home from FAMU and got my job back at Sears, I was working in sales. After some time, I got promoted to work in the group office. For the first couple of months, I did the menial tasks until they figured out that I was actually a smart person. Then they discovered that I had worked in high school as a news writer and was writing for my church bulletin. Our church had a newsletter at that time called the "Evangelistic News," and I was the co-editor. After learning this, they tried to see whether I could write ads using the procedural book as my style guide. It turned out that I was not only a good copy writer, but I was also the best writer they had. Ultimately, I became the copyright chief for Sears Roebuck.

After more than five years, I was promoted to personnel manager at Sears, which is now called human resources manager, and I made sure that blacks always had the opportunity to not only be recognized and identified, but also to be elevated. My first role as a Sears personnel manager was in West Palm Beach, Florida, in 1973, where I worked for two years. When I got there, it was shortly after further affirmative action efforts had been taken by President Nixon. Although the affirmative action legislation only affected federal agencies and contracting, Sears had adopted the notion of making sure that they were in line with national efforts. My job was to ensure that, at every level I was responsible for, there was minority representation. I took this very seriously, and I loved it. I superimposed blacks in every department I could. For instance, I took hardworking black people from the service station and made them salespeople.

One of my best friends, the late Ed Ganzy, who later became a member of my church, followed me my entire career at Sears. Once I got him promoted out of the Sears coffee shop as the head cook, I made him a store manager. He was not just a manager, though—he was an operations manager. He would close the store at night and had his own set of keys to everything. When I transferred to Atlanta, Georgia, Buckhead store in 1975, I went overboard to ensure that I identified and promoted as many promising black people as possible. I not only hired blacks, but also whites. One of those hires was James "Chip" Carter, son of former U.S. President Jimmy Carter. I hired him to work in the service station at Sears Roebuck.

I moved from a management position to a sales position in big ticket items so I could make more money. Against the advice of the store manager, Porter McClean, I started in sales in May 1985. I quickly became the number one salesperson in the department, selling more washers and dryers, microwaves, and refrigerators than anyone else. The following year, which would be my last year at Sears, I was number three in the Sears system nationwide in number of units sold.

I worked at Sears for 20 years. Like my father, I had made a career of it because I loved it, but I also loved pastoring. When the two came into conflict as far as my time and attention, I knew I had to let Sears go and focus on ministry full time, which is the same decision my father had made years before. Daddy had started pastoring in 1965. Prior to that, he was an evangelist, or associate minister, and he didn't earn any type of income from the church. Once he began pastoring full time and working at Sears, the two roles kept overlapping. He was required on one and he was requested on the other. Ultimately, he just couldn't do it anymore, so he reluctantly decided to let Sears go, as preaching was what he loved. The same thing happened to me.

20

BACK TO BAPTIST

Shortly after returning to Miami in 1977 after living in Atlanta, Georgia, for almost two years, I was invited to apply for the minister of music position at the Second Baptist Church. The Reverend John A. Ferguson had approached me about becoming a part of his ministerial staff. He wanted to name me as "Minister of Music" and "Minister of Education."

I had worked at Second Baptist Church of Richmond Heights, Florida, as a musical director for the youth choir in 1972 when I separated from my military obligations. The choir was filled with 20 wonderfully talented young singers at the time, such as the Johnson sisters: Phyllis, Pat and Corliss. I truly loved developing them. I would perform with the choir once per month while still playing at my father's church at other times.

Rev. Ferguson's dad was a member of the Church of God of Prophecy, where my great-uncle TJ was the bishop, so they knew each other well from the church. When my great uncle built the church in 1943 and needed some work to be done, Rev. Ferguson's dad did handiwork and carpentry, including stucco work. So, when I came home from the military in May 1972, a few people asked me to be a part of their ministry because of my musical ability. Rev. Ferguson found out that I was back home and got in touch with me through my relatives who went to my dad's church. He said he needed some help at his church, so I accepted a position working with the youth choir at Second Baptist for the year.

I was also working at Sears' Biscayne location, but they soon promoted me from that store to the new Cutler Ridge Mall store, nearly 40 miles away. I became a training manager and was responsible for training all the new employees. Sears had a program in which they identified black talent from around the country and brought them to Miami to be future managers, and I was responsible for training them all.

If I took the new position Rev. Ferguson was offering, I would be training and working with many of the same young people whom I taught in the youth choir five years previously. I discussed this offer with my father under a shady tree in his front yard. He tearfully requested that I reconsider being absent from the church on Sundays to attend another church. He offered to pay me whatever I was going to make at Second Baptist. I told my father in a respectful but bold way that I was obeying the voice of the Lord and would take the position offered at Second Baptist.

I tendered a letter of resignation to the Tabernacle and asked my daddy to read it to the congregation. I'm not sure whether the letter was ever read, but the situation was brought before the church during a Sunday morning worship service, where my father led the church to excommunicate me from Tabernacle. I was told shortly afterwards that the ushers and men were advised that if I visited the church, I was to sit in the audience and not in the pulpit.

At Second Baptist, my musical responsibilities focused on directing the young adult choir, whose members had to be at least 14 years old. One youngster, Patrice, was allowed to join the choir at age 12 or so because she was big for her age and could really sing. When the choir travelled to Philadelphia, Pennsylvania, to sing in 1980 at the Gospel Music workshop of America, Patrice carried a baby doll on the trip. In less than a year of full-time work with the young adult choir, we became a leading gospel music entity in the South Florida church community. Among the main soloists was Berthina Jones, a poised alto with great vocal range. An audience favorite was when she led the song "God Is," written by James Cleveland. Compared to my family's lively Pentecostal worship style, Second Baptist had a rather reserved congregation during praise and worship—that is, until Berthina would begin softly singing the words:

> *God is*
> *My protection*
> *God is*
> *My all and all*

In the Key of M

As I played the organ and the choir joined chorus with *God is the joy and the strength of my life; (God is) He removes all pain misery and strife; (God is) He promised to keep me; Never to leave me,* the entire congregation would be on its feet. The song would go on for nearly 10 minutes or more, invoking a powerful corporate praise. Performance of that song and other rousing tunes became a hallmark for the choir and ultimately the church.

I went on to accompany and perform with the Miami Mass Choir in 1978 under the direction of Lehman Beneby. Later, under the direction of Rev. Arthur T. Jones and Earl B. Mason, the choir recorded and produced two songs under Savoy Records, earning Grammy nominations. Over the next two years, I was nominated for two Grammy Awards for the following:

Florida Mass Choir — "Come Let Us Reason Together" (1979)
Rev. Walter Richardson soloist, Savoy Records

The Atlanta Philharmonic Chorale & John W. Griggs — "I Am Thine, O Lord" (1980) featuring Rev. Walter Richardson, Accent Records

While the music ministry was soaring and membership was growing, Rev. Ferguson, more than anything else, became focused on my formal education. He wanted to know whether I had finished my education, but I had not. "Well, you got to go back to school," he insisted. "You got to help me. You got to help your dad. You got to help us. You got to help the ministry. We are in Miami, a very large place, and most of the Baptist ministers here don't have a formal education in ministry or counseling. That's inexcusable."

At the time, I didn't understand his insistence, but soon I would come to see his point of view. In 1981, there was a counseling course being offered at Biscayne College that he wanted me to take. He said, "You've got to take this course. You've got to get back in school and do what you can do to help our people." At age 58, he felt it was too late for him to go back to school, but he truly believed in me.

When it was time for me to go to school as he suggested, he explained, "You know why I want you to go to school and take this course in counseling?"

I replied, "I have an idea you want me to further my education so I can be of greater assistance to you."

"No," he said. "I had a very bad experience that I have to live with for the rest of my life. I gave somebody bad advice." Then he went about retelling the story of a young woman who came to see him after church one Sunday. She was a member at Second Baptist and served as an usher. He described her usher's uniform as looking wrinkled. He said it was noticeable that she had not ironed it before she came to church, which was unlike her because she was always nice and neat. As she was talking, he realized that she had taken that dress with her wherever she went after she left her husband that Tuesday. She took her usher uniform because she knew she was going to be gone at least through Sunday. She asked to see him after church. She explained that she left her house because her husband had jumped on her and fought her earlier in the week.

"No man's gonna ever do that to me," she told Rev. Ferguson. "But you're my pastor. Whatever you tell me to do, I'm prepared to do it."

"Let's pray," he advised after some time.

After they prayed together, he said, "I believe the Lord wants me to tell you to go back home to your husband. Everything is going to be alright."

Later that Sunday afternoon, while he was having dinner, his adult daughter called him and said, "Daddy, you need to come around to my house now." She and her family lived near her parents, in the same area, and she lived across the street from the woman he had counseled earlier that day. She had no idea about the conversation her father'd had with this woman. She just told her dad that he needed to get around to her house so that he could tell her how she should respond, because there was a lot of police activity at the lady's house.

So Rev. Ferguson drove over to his daughter's house, and he immediately saw the brigade of police and an ambulance. After speaking with police and bystanders, he found out that when she went back home to her husband, he killed her.

"Waller," he said, which is what he called me, "I have to live with that for the rest of my life. I thought I was doing the right thing because I prayed, but I didn't have the counseling skills to deal with that situation. I didn't know I could refer her to someone. I didn't know."

In the Key of M

He explained that that was why I needed to take the counseling course. "You need to take this course and get some training, so not only are you able to preach, but you'll also be able to pastor. You'll know when you need to refer people to another professional agency. You need to be a fully-equipped pastor, not just know how to sing and play, but know how to pastor people and take care of their social *and* their spiritual problems."

Rev. Ferguson was very active in the Richmond Heights community. Some elite families from Bethel Baptist helped him organize the Second Baptist Church, and many of them were educators and businesspeople. Rev. Ferguson was involved in the desegregation of many of the county's facilities and workplaces, and he worked diligently for equality in education. He was a member of the first county community relations board and represented South Dade. Most of the other members of the CRB came from Miami. The Reverend Edward Graham, pastor of the historic Mt. Zion Baptist Church, was very active in politics and civil rights issues. Coconut Grove had civil rights advocacy from people like Father Theodore Gibson, but Richmond Heights was a new area for blacks that had not been around before 1950. The other major congregations, Glendale Baptist Church and Martin Memorial African Methodist Episcopal Church, had leadership that was mostly involved in denominational activities, but the community needs were not being addressed in corporate ways.

When I got back to Second Baptist in 1977, Rev. Ferguson thoroughly trained and taught me, pushing me out front to preach because I was a gifted speaker. He sensed I had a great calling and had a vision for what I was going to be doing while he was able to mentor me. He treated me like a son, offering both personal and professional direction. Shortly after I became a member of the staff at Second Baptist Church, Reverend Ferguson introduced me to the leaders of local church organizations and had me meet with all of them to learn denominational structures. He also introduced me to other county community leaders so that I was taught the system of county government. As a direct result of his leadership and involvement with me, I joined him as a member of the Metro Miami Action Plan (MMAP) on the advisory board, where we made selections to the board. He also urged me to join the Dade County Community Relations Board. While many of the black congregations in and around Miami had good church leadership, very few pastors were considered influential in government or public school matters like Rev. Ferguson.

As I started to do more community work, all kinds of attention came my way — some good and some not so good. It's no secret that women are attracted to famous or successful men just as successful men are oftentimes attracted to young, beautiful women. Research has shown, in fact, that women find a man more attractive if other women think so, or if the man is already in a relationship (Street, et al. 2018). Women in the church are no different. As a popular minister and musician, I have seen and experienced how women are drawn to pastors. I saw it when I was growing up in my father's small church and how certain women would be extra friendly. My father was, as far as I know, respectful and never crossed the line with women in the church or community. Of course, people always conjured rumors about who they thought was flirting or possibly "stepping out." As my own popularity grew in the church, I was confronted with the same temptations and flirtations as my father but on a greater scale because of my national affiliations.

My first, real challenge in this regard occurred in 1980, when I was working and traveling a lot to perform with the mass choir. I was having some issues in my marriage, but as usual, work was my therapeutic escape. Being incredibly ambitious and dedicated to my craft, I was always working, and I loved it. However, this strained my family and likely made my wife feel like a single parent at times. She was struggling with her health, so my routine absence compounded things, as she was looking for greater companionship and support. I, perhaps, may have also encouraged any insecurities she had by being too friendly and gratuitous with compliments of other women, especially those younger than she. As an extrovert, I gravitate to people, but my wife is more reserved and introverted. While she has always understood this about me, my carefree interactions with flirty women probably made her uncomfortable. I needed to be more metered in my interactions, but I hadn't matured in that regard as yet.

I spent a lot of time practicing with the choir in preparation for our performances, and during this time, I began having extended conversations after rehearsal with one woman. As it says in 1 Corinthians 7:5, we cannot deprive ourselves in marriage for an extended time without fasting and prayer, because Satan will come to tempt you. As believers, especially as a pastor, we cannot give Satan any opportunities (Eph. 4:27), and this is what happened in this situation. As a result of infidelity, my son Robert Brown was born December 1980. I paid child support for him, and I did try to be part of his life. He looks a lot like me, and he even began preaching for a time. Although he is no longer working in the ministry and pursuing other career interests, I am quite proud of the respectful, kind person he is.

21

HOME SWEET HOME

I was invited to apply for the position of pastor at Sweet Home Missionary
Baptist Church in 1983. Reverend James Allen had resigned as pastor,
and my name had been mentioned by Ruthie Simmons, the daughter-
in-law of the chairman of the deacon board at the church, as a possible
candidate. Ruthie was also a personnel assistant at the Sears store where
I worked, and I had sung at her daughter's funeral service. Ironically, Sis.
Bertha Collins at Second Baptist was the daughter-in-law of one of the
founders of Sweet Home, Deacon Collins, and when approached, she
thought the church could not find a better fit for the new pastor.

I met with the deacons and trustees to share my vision of what a church
should be. The field of candidates was narrowed to two after some months,
and the church had the choice between me and Rev. Joe Lewis, a classic
Baptist preacher with a strong singing and preaching voice. He was a major
whooper and sounded a lot like the legendary C. L. Franklin. I received a
phone call on the second Wednesday in October 1983 at about 9:30 p.m.
that the church had voted to extend the offer to me to become the pastor.

My father had ordained me to preach in May 1971, but Rev. Ferguson
ordained me again on November 19, 1983. Even though I was a pastor, I
had been an assistant to Rev. Ferguson, and the fact that I was ordained in
a Pentecostal church did not hold weight in a Baptist church. Furthermore,
being the pastor of Sweet Home was a responsibility that required
ordination, and I wanted to ensure everything was official. I would be the
legitimate, ordained pastor of Sweet Home.

The church was established around February 1952 by several deacons
and area ministers. The congregation started meeting initially out of a

school while the church building was being built. During construction, they moved to a church that was already built where they could split services. They would worship there in the morning, and the holiness congregation would hold worship services in the afternoon. They referenced the building as "Doc Coleman's church." I don't know the real name of the church, but Doc Coleman, a local civic leader, was the pastor. It was a Pentecostal church, and they ended up calling it Bible Way Apostolic Church (or something like that) once the Baptist congregation stopped having services there. When the new church building was finished, they moved from there into their permanent facility in Perrine, naming it Sweet Home Missionary Baptist Church at 17201 103rd Avenue, Miami, FL 33157. All this happened in 1952, and Reverend Elzie King served as the first pastor for 22 years.

I preached my first sermon as pastor of Sweet Home in October 1983. I was officially installed as pastor on January 15, 1984, on Martin Luther King, Jr.'s birthday. We held church services twice per month, on second and fourth Sundays, but Sunday School was conducted every week. Initially, I was trying to pastor and work at Sears at the same time, because I had no choice. My salary when I first started at Sweet Home was $383 a month, and the $83 was designated for food. Broken down, I was earning $150 every other week for pastoring and $41.50 for food. It was slightly more than I had been getting at Second Baptist, which was paying me $333 a month as the minister of music. This covered Wednesday night rehearsal and the Sunday performance for two services.

After my first full year as pastor of Sweet Home, we were still having church services twice per month, despite the fact that the church was growing rapidly. For Easter Sunday that year, we had an exchange service with Morningstar Baptist Church in Goulds, Florida. Sweet Home had to go to Morningstar to do the early sunrise service where I would preach, and it was on a first Sunday. We had such a good fellowship with that church, and when the services were over towards the end, I made an announcement. I said, "Listen, we've had such a good time here. This is Easter Sunday, and for me, it doesn't make sense that we leave this service and just go home. My family and I are going to leave here and we're going to go to Sweet Home Baptist Church. If there's nobody there but me and my family, that's okay. We've got to give God praise on Easter Sunday at Sweet Home Baptist Church at 11 o'clock." There was an explosion of applause.

In the Key of M

I didn't know what was going to happen, but I just knew I had to make that announcement. We had just had service the previous week, on the fourth Sunday, and now this was first Sunday. We had never done this before, but I was determined.

By the time my wife and I got to Sweet Home's parking lot, it was packed. People were waiting there for service. We walked in to have Easter service with no plan or program, but everything turned out well. The following Sunday was second, and we were going to have church as scheduled. During that service, I made a declaration similar to what I had announced on Easter Sunday. "Hey, y'all, for three straight weeks now we've had service. We've had service for fourth Sunday. We've had service for first Sunday on Easter, and now here we are for the second Sunday. You know what we ought to do? We ought to come back next Sunday and have church for third Sunday."

I didn't run this suggestion by the deacon board or anybody else. Led by the Spirit, I just made the announcement. Afterwards, I did get some pushback. There were some who said, "You can't just do that. This needs to go before the conference."

I responded, saying, "We'll be here next Sunday. If you don't want to come, you don't have to come, but I have the keys. If I have to play, you know, if there's a budget challenge because we got to pay a musician, I can play. That's not going to be a problem." Sweet Home has had church service every Sunday since that declaration, and that was in April 1985.

Meanwhile, taking care of funerals, weddings, counseling sessions, meetings and hospitalized members—all the pastoral responsibilities— became a little bit too much while still working. I eventually retired from Sears in December 1986 when the church was able to pay me to be a full-time pastor. I had given the company 20 years of dedicated service, but I looked forward to giving the church my full-time attention. Knowing I would need adequate resources and support, I asked the church to buy a computer and hire a secretary for me. The church's first secretary, Pat Hearns, also worked part time as a school bus driver, so she could only work between 10 a.m. and 2 p.m. every day. My income was doubled from $15,000 to $30,000 per year, which was less than one-third of what I was earning at Sears. I then started teaching music part-time at Miami Dade College's Kendall campus, earning about $1,000 per month, to supplement my salary at Sweet Home. Music wasn't a job to me, though. It was a calling, like preaching.

Sweet Home began growing by leaps and bounds around this time. We held services in the original wooden church until the congregation grew to a point where we were overcrowded by 1989. Because the church could only hold 115 people, including 100 in the audience and 15 in the choir, we had to have multiple services every Sunday. We were faced with having to construct an entirely new building. Originally, we contracted a black architect, Ron Frazier, to design the new church. He drew up an impressive design, but it was very expensive and didn't match the community's needs. After several meetings, we thanked him and told him we were going to explore other options. Someone recommended that we go with Mursten Construction. The owner was a white man named Harry Mursten, but we were told that he was dedicated to helping the less fortunate. Apparently, he was a wealthy man who had done well in the construction industry, and he had an affinity for building churches (Cohen 2016). Once we contracted his company, Harry explained that not only would he design a facility that complemented the neighborhood, but he would also ensure that it was constructed well and provided savings wherever he could in the process. The church ended up saving almost half a million dollars from the original estimate. We borrowed $1.5 million from the bank and raised the other half million ourselves. Thus, the total outlay for the project was approximately $2 million, and it took two years.

We moved into the new church building in August 1991. The new facility could hold about 600, but our first service had over 900 attendees there. We had to put extra chairs in the aisles and in an overflow area near the foyer. Typically, we would have two services on Sundays: one at 7:30 a.m. and then one at 11 a.m. Those services got so packed, though, that we ended up actually having three services on some occasions, hosting an additional one at 9:30 a.m. Eventually, we had to turn folks away because there were just too many people. They couldn't even get in the building, and those who could get in, couldn't find a place to sit. We then made plans to build a new, larger facility. The new church held its first service on January 11, 2009, and we did so in grand fashion with a motorcade from the site of the old building to the new building. Located at *10701 S.W. 184th Street, Cutler Bay, Florida*, about one mile from the previous location, it was built on 24 acres of land, and the church building could hold about 2,000 people.

In the Key of M

No matter where we worshipped throughout the years, the heart of Sweet Home remained the same: a focus on community impact. One of the first things I said to the deacon board is that "this church is in a good location." I felt that you can't really have a good church and a bad community. I added, "This is a bad community, so we are not a good church. Because the same people that make up a community make up our church, we must do something about changing this environment." At the time, Perrine was plagued with crime ushered in by a drug epidemic and poverty. People were getting shot, stabbed, and robbed on a regular basis, and gangs had taken over parts of the community. People were gambling on every street corner, and prostitution was rampant. Meanwhile, Sweet Home was calling itself a "good church."

My disagreement with that notion was vocal and consistent, but my dedication to change and community impact was just as passionate. "We can't be a good church just yet," I said, "because the same people who are doing these crimes are connected to people inside the church. Some of them are even benefiting from the sins of their kids. To be a good church, we've got to get involved in the community. Once we figure out what we want our community to look like, then we have to engage the larger community in the county to help us."

One of the first people to help me adequately address our community was Janet Reno, who was friends with Rev. Ferguson. Reno was serving as State Attorney for Dade County at the time and was the first woman to serve in this position. The three of us made some changes in tandem, organizing and starting a group called the West Perrine Christian Association following the death of a local grocer named Lee Arthur Lawrence in March 1989. Lawrence was an outspoken community crusader who tried to expel drug and related criminal activity in the West Perrine community near his store (Dellagloria 2008). Apparently, two men carrying Uzi submachine guns and wearing military fatigues gunned down the 52-year-old man in front of his convenience store, which had previously been the target of attempted arson (Bell 1989). This was a tipping point in the community and became an opportunity to coalesce other voices who would decry the rising crime and demand change.

People in the neighborhood knew how Lawrence had pleaded for help from the police and elected officials to rid the front of his store (and the entire community) of drugs and other illicit activity. After his death, I got the church involved. We marched through the community every Saturday. I would lead the March along with my secretary at the time, Dennis Moss, who is now a retired county commissioner. We were organized and super-charged, and as a result, we picked up a few residents, maybe a couple dozen or so, who would join us along the way. By the time we stopped marching, we had several hundred people who had started marching through the streets of West Perrine with us. White churches even joined us as we marched each Saturday against drugs and crime in our neighbor-hoods, and it helped. County and police officials took notice and interven-tions began to take place.

As our presence in the community grew, so did the diversity. The congre-gation went from being mainly African-American middle-aged and older folks to having a robust young adult, more culturally diverse presence. In fact, almost half of our young adult ministry were students from University of Miami because our young adult pastor was the chaplain for the sports teams, so we had black and white college football players attend along with members of the track team. I put the black law students from UM in leadership positions. We did a wonderful job of attracting young pro-fessionals. We had professional football players such as Lawrence Taylor, basketball players such as Glen Rice, actors, actresses and the like join the church, and they were supportive financially.

About 5 percent of the congregation were from other racial or cultural groups with an appreciable amount of people from the Caribbean. Meanwhile, First Baptist Church in Perrine, which was historically an all-white church, was increasing its Caribbean footprint, and they were proud of that. The pastor at the time, Tommy Watson, would assert the fact that he had more Caribbean blacks at his church than most all the local black churches combined, such as Second Baptist, Glendale, and Sweet Home. He saw his church as *the* melting pot within the community, but we saw ours as the community conscious.

22

COMMUNITY CLERIC

As we continued to combat community challenges, we did not do so haphazardly. We had a 17-point plan, drawn up by the West Perrine Community Development Corporation (CDC), the civic group founded by Edward Hanna. Hanna was a member of the West Perrine Christian Association as well, and we teamed together to confront issues both directly and indirectly. He was at every march with us as we confronted the bad guys who were actively selling drugs, gambling, and so forth. We were not afraid of them. We would actually stop in front of places of ill repute to minister the Word of God and pray with them. Our marching had another goal beyond letting people know that we were united in our reform efforts, but to redeem lost souls. Furthermore, we wanted the bad guys to realize that the number of good people in the community would always outnumber them. We were also going to let them know we loved them but their illicit activity had to cease.

Part of the 17-point plan was to have revival. The bad guys were invited, and some of them actually converted. Many people got saved, in fact, as a result of what we were doing in the community. They respected us because we had the capacity and the audacity to confront them and tell them how we felt about it. We didn't just talk about them; we talked to them. The plan was effective because it was comprehensive, touching on everything from the school system to employment opportunities.

As the association president and spokesperson, I was the one who went to the county commission meetings and made research and reality-based presentations. I had the support of not only my church congregation, but I was also backed by other local pastors who would bring their congregations.

Many times, we would pack the chamber as I spoke about the changes we needed to make our community viable. I talked about overgrown lots, domestic violence, and churches coming together with one voice.

We had personally seen the results of our intervention in the King family, who owned the Cab Stand. It was a place that was known for being a magnet for nightclub activity and, eventually, criminal activity. Although the King family may not have been directly involved, you could go to the Cab Stand and buy stolen jewelry, guns, or whatever. Prostitution, like other crimes, had also begun to proliferate there. I was able to witness one of the King family members not only get saved, but also become a minister in my church.

Before we got involved the way we did, stolen cars were a regular occurrence. Criminals had a place to take the car, strip it and get it back on the streets with little obstruction. The West Perrine community went from an average of 22 stolen cars per week at the height of the '80s crime spree to zero once we became active. You couldn't bring a stolen car to Perrine because we had it on lockdown.

We had empowered our community with help from people like Janet Reno, the first woman to serve as state attorney in Florida, who came up with this idea of empowering the community to heal itself by engaging professionals in law enforcement, the medical profession, social work, and education. We started out with a police officer named Ron Tookes, who is still there working in the community. Evelyn Harris was a nurse who joined us, and she's still in the area, too. We had a social worker named Matthew Price, but we also wanted to add a schoolteacher. We had just three people, but the initial mission was to have four people go door to door until every household was identified. A survey was to be taken of every household to find out what their needs were, and we were to provide follow-up services through the county systems to which they were attached. So, if we discovered one home where there was substance abuse, we identified local support services, and we would follow-up and work with that family until they could overcome it. If the problem was economic, we found a way to help with that. If it was continual interaction with law enforcement in a negative way, we found a way through our police representative to take care of that. We even started programs specifically geared to help those witnessing or facing immediate crises. We had a hotline set up so that if people who stayed in public housing could anonymously communicate with law enforcement about criminal activity they saw. We knew we were getting relevant information that could only come from people in that environment, and it worked to keep the neighborhoods safer. At that time, people who supported us weren't considered "snitches"—they were considered "community healers." We had some good outcomes overall, but the campaign didn't last that long because we got some pushback. Nevertheless, we did get some notoriety in the form of community awards and media interviews. While recognition is always nice, our aim started out and remained squarely focused on results. Our victories were cyclical for sure, though. We would get a victory here, and then something would come along and wipe that victory away.

Despite the setbacks, my determination never waned throughout the years. At one point, there were no blacks and leadership with the YMCA. So the blacks in the area, particularly in the Liberty City area, formed their own youth community group. They had the same programs as the YMCA, including fine arts, where they taught piano. I was a product of that effort. When I moved to South Dade and became the pastor at Sweet Home. I recognized that the YMCA offered lots of activities, but only to those on the other side of the Dixie Highway, which was predominately white. They offered nothing in Richmond Heights or Perrine. A few others and I grew curious about the separation and confronted the organization, letting them know that we wanted to be a part of it because we had black residents in the South Dade community that needed the services. Curtis Lawrence, owner of Henry Dry Cleaning, was instrumental in getting me and others like Wilbur Bell involved. We stayed engaged with the organization, ensuring that black youth could participate, and when it was time for a change in leadership, my name was mentioned. I became the first black president of the South Dade branch of the YMCA in 2002. While in office, I helped to secure a new building for the YMCA, which is a first-class center located at *9355 SW 134th Street*. As a result of the being on the South Dade board, as their president, I was asked to be a part of the general board of YMCA.

Organized by several local pastors, People United to Lead the Struggle for Equality (PULSE) was the local version of the NAACP. It was a Miami-based organization but had some extensions a little further into northern Broward County. The organization was interested in any areas in which blacks faced inequality or were struggling, whether it be in employment, law enforcement, or even domestic affairs. The late Reverend Dr. Arthur Jackson, Jr. was the president, and he led the organization that did a lot of work to empower black folks in Dade County. It, in fact, became like a go-to organization for community activism because Rev. Jackson had a strong connection with the local State Attorney's Office, led, at that time, by Janet Reno. She was very much involved in supporting racial equality and social justice efforts. When it was time for us to tackle the issue of immigration for Haitians, because they were not given the privilege as the Cubans had to get close to America and become immediately eligible for citizenship, PULSE went to lobby and meet senators and representatives in Washington. We went on a bus as part of that delegation in 2003. The late Rev. Emmanuel Whipple, Sr. was my roommate and writing partner while we were there in D.C. We went door to door, to each member of Congress we could engage, talking about the need for immigration reform for Haitians.

I was a part of another group in 2005 that went over to see the living conditions in Haiti firsthand. Years before, in 1993, I had personally joined a Krome sympathy hunger strike along with about 160 others, including members of the NAACP such as general counsel David Honig, to demand more "humane treatment" of Haitian immigrants being detained (Viglucci 1993). Haitian detainees held at Krome Avenue Detention Center accused INS authorities of mistreatment after 48 Cuban defectors who had diverted a Cuban airliner to Miami were quickly released. The Haitians who remained locked up at the center west of Miami demanded the same treatment (Martin 1993).

This time, we were actually in Haiti to provide assistance, assess the level of poverty, provide economic development ideas, and bring the Gospel to Haiti. On a practical level, our project included trying to identify places where we could put in wells because clean water was lacking and deforestation was rampant. We saw some very unsightly places where people were actually burning trees to start small open fires in order to cook or even boil water. The people's need was great and immediate. We visited one of the most destitute places in Haiti called Titiyan, which was a former burial ground just outside Port-au-Prince. We saw young girls prostituting themselves to men in the same neighborhood in order to get money for them and their families. We stayed there for a week and once I returned home, I preached about the experience. Our church actually adopted a family in Haiti. As a result of what was going on with this particular mission group, many kids were able to leave Haiti and come to the United States for school. Many families were also able to relocate to the U.S. as a result of the work we were doing. There were some missionaries already working there as well, and they were doing great work. Our church made a way to support them financially.

23

GOING BACK TO SCHOOL

I had been prompted by Rev. Ferguson to get as much education as I could so I would not only be a learned contributor to people in the church and local community, but also to a wider audience. I was always interested and involved in social action and wanted to see my communities empowered and motivated to bring about more social healing, economic improvement, and educational opportunities. Of the institutions that offered the kind of education I desired, the only one that offered me a scholarship because I was a minister was the same school where I received my bachelor's degree, St. Thomas University.

The Master of Arts degree in Pastoral Ministry was a 36-hour program of study, and I began the summer after finishing my undergraduate degree in 1987. The reading was intense and the writing requirements were stringent. As I was the lone black in my class, the professors all paid extra attention to my pursuits, and helped to individually hone my skills. Dr. Mary Carter Warren was passionate about civic engagement, and after having the class read "Habits of the Heart," spent lots of time mentoring me in the ways of social activism within the Roman Catholic Church. I was exposed to the liberation movement in Latin America and found tremendous overlap in the experiences of blacks in America and Latinos in South America. I took a full load of classes, including two summers, and by December of 1989, I had completed my studies, examinations and all.

Simultaneous to my engagement with the master's program, I had applied for doctoral studies. I took the GRE and placed several schools on my testing material as places I would love to receive my scores. Among them were the Harvard, Yale, and Duke Divinity Schools. I had considered briefly attending Nova University, but they did not offer courses in Religion. The only approximate discipline I was interested in was psychology. I was encouraged to apply to Harvard and Duke and was excited; however, there was a major problem. The board of my church did not want to see me out of the pulpit and wanted me available for pastoral responsibilities. So, while they were happy that I was considering pursuing my doctorate degree, they were more concerned about my absence. To appease them, I applied to the University of Miami for the Ph.D. program in philosophy. I was immediately accepted and given a full scholarship, and along with three other students who were likewise given scholarships, began our studies in August 1989. The reading requirements were at least double to those in my Master's program, and with one semester left at St. Thomas to complete my studies, I literally had no time to prepare a sermon on Sundays. I studied in the mornings from around 5 to 7 a.m., assisted my wife with early morning details after that, and then left for classes. Since my scholarship indicated I was to be available as a graduate assistant, I also had to spend extra time on campus grading papers for my professors. As chance would have it, beginning January 1990, I began teaching my own class because the professor to whom I was assigned had to take some time off because of a tragic death. I taught introduction to philosophy to undergraduates, and as time went on, I began teaching religion. This deepened my own under-standing of religion's historical impact on society, and it helped me better grasp the gravity and potential legacy of my own role in church leadership. I discovered that I loved teaching like music. In fact, it is a similitude of preaching that includes direct feedback and debate.

24

THE STORM

Dolores and I were on vacation in Orlando and heard that a hurricane was approaching Miami. We were neither concerned about our property nor the safety of our family, because the news reports in Orlando did not suggest that the weather situation in Miami was critical. We also hadn't heard from family members living in Miami about the storm's severity or any damage it had done while traveling across the Atlantic.

The only reason Dolores and I decided to return to Miami on August 23, 1992, was because Kathy, a member of our church, asked me to perform her marriage to Charles Wright in the yard of her mother's home. It was a small wedding with only immediate family members and a few friends. After the wedding, around 5 p.m., we rushed home to secure our house. I was surprised when I went to the stores that all the water, batteries, and food stuff had been purchased. I was afraid to also discover that all building material to cover windows and doors had been purchased. Desperate, I found some sturdy cardboard and masking tape to cover my windows. Around 7 p.m., I received a phone call from one of my associate ministers, Victor Grubbs, who told me he had nowhere safe to spend the night–he had been directed by the Air Force to vacate his military housing. Even more troubling was the fact that his wife, Joyce, had just two days prior delivered their second child, and she had to vacate the military hospital because they expected a direct strike from the hurricane on Homestead Air Force Base.

We had LaKisha give up her room to share her brother's bedroom, and we gave Victor, his wife, young daughter, and the newborn baby our daughter's bedroom. Honestly, I never expected what happened next. As the night wore on, strong winds began to howl outside, and there was some heavy but occasional rain. Both my family and the Grubbses slept while I stayed awake listening, wondering, and worrying about what was happening outside. I heard objects being thrown around outside. The lights flickered and then went out for a few minutes. Then all of a sudden, I heard my roof cracking, and I ran to my son's room to discover that he had a serious leak in the ceiling. So, I got him and his sister up and had them come to our bedroom. I don't' remember whether the wind was louder or the pounding rain. I grabbed my flashlight since the lights were out again and checked on our guests. They were still asleep, exhausted from having to pack and leave the Homestead Air Force Base. Within minutes, the leak worsened and spread to the Grubbses' bedroom, and then to the master bedroom, where my wife, still sleeping, started awake, feeling that something was terribly wrong.

I pulled the top mattress of our queen-sized mattress into the living room area, ordered Victor and his family to get to the living room and cover themselves on one of the sofas. I yelled for our children to get on the other sofa, but to stay close to their mother while I went through the house trying to cover and move furniture, clothes, and items that were getting wet because of the cracks in the ceiling and now completely broken roof. The storm intensified—the wind blew and broke the large front window, and the water from the rain and the force of the window threatened our safety as we hovered nearby in the living room. To reduce the effects of the wind and rain coming through that window, I rolled the recently-purchased six-foot grand piano over to the window and lifted it on the side to cover the window area. My daughter watched in horror, yelling and crying. My son could not help me because he was making sure the others, especially his mother, were okay. In what seemed like an entire night's episode, minutes later, after a few more squalls, the worst was over even though the wind and rain continued. And now, without electricity, all we could do was pray and wait to see what would develop when the sun came up.

When morning came, we went through the house to survey the damage. All three of the bedrooms were completely destroyed from floor to roof. The furniture had been blown around, closets broken, clothes strewn around the room, and valuables, jewelry, and the family computer, were soaked and covered with pieces of pinkish roofing insulation. A large piece

In the Key of M

of wood, either from our neighbor's yard or somewhere close, had pierced the window over our daughter's bedroom. Had anyone still been there, someone could have died. The living room area was similarly wet. All of us walked around the house as if visiting a museum and shaking our heads in disbelief. There was no electricity, and there would be no electricity for weeks to come.

Joyce and Dolores discussed how to feed the children, and Victor hung around to determine his next move. I asked my son to help me open the broken garage, and we then looked outside. It looked like we were in a different part of the world. It was difficult to see the street because it looked like an extension of everyone's yards. Water, debris, damaged lawn furniture, boats, electrical wires, street signs, trees and limbs, strewn leaves, and wooden boards covered the landscape of our block. The sounds of sirens from house alarms, emergency vehicles, rescue helicopters, and screaming neighbors filled the air. The atmosphere was eerie and surreal. No air conditioners were running, no dogs barking, no typical noise. Except for the sirens and conversations, it was totally silent and completely still outdoors. Of the trees standing or uprooted, none of them had leaves.

After talking for a few minutes with neighbors, all of whom experienced similar damage and destruction of their property, I backed my car from the garage and asked my son to accompany me on what I thought would be a quick trip to the church. We passed three houses to get to the corner of our block, turning left to advance towards the main street to the church. We noticed several cars had tried to leave the neighborhood by traveling through yards to get around the debris in the streets. As we got close to the edge of our development, a small crowd had gathered in front of one neighbor's yard. Some people were on the ground, leaning over a man who was obviously sick or injured. I got out of my car to determine the nature of the situation, only to learn that the man was already dead. I tried on my police radio to get on the air, but found that there were no police communications. With no help in sight, with no communication services, two neighbors decided to take the deceased man to the hospital in their car.

I proceeded through our development to the main street that accessed the church where I pastored. After driving around fallen trees, debris, and electric wires, I managed to get into the parking lot of Sweet Home. The alarm was still faintly ringing. From the outside I could tell that the stained glass was damaged, but not broken. My son and I struggled to get to the door to open the office. The entrance had been beaten up so badly that the lock was almost inoperable. We walked slowly around the building. The large exterior glass windows to the church meeting room were all broken, and the roof was severely damaged. After we entered the church through the office doors, we saw that the secretary's area and the pastor's office had been destroyed by wind and water, and the interior walls had been pushed out of place. The main sanctuary was completely covered in water about an inch deep, and the air conditioning unit, which was housed on the ceiling of the sanctuary, had fallen onto the pews. The church building had been recently dedicated, having been built only one year earlier, almost to the day. The Hammond organ and speaker were wet. The new six-foot Kawai piano, purchased the same time as my personal piano, was also wet. The new hymn books were wet, but nothing had been stolen. The phones were working, so I tried to contact some men from the church to alert them to the need to secure the windows to avoid theft.

Initially, the Miami Dade Police Department put my family up at Marco Polo Hotel in Miami Beach. I was the only chaplain for the police department at that time, though they now have more than ten. During the period of the storm, we had lost two chaplains. One died and one retired. The police department never brought anybody else on to be a chaplain, so when the storm hit, I was the only one. They housed all the command staff, including the chaplain, in Marco Polo Hotel. Although we were located temporarily away from the action and trauma of the area, we had to commute every day by caravan down to the South Dade area to do our work with the police department.

We stayed at the hotel for a few days until we decided to stay with my father in Opa-locka, who still lived in the same house that I was raised in. While we were surely welcome there, my family had to sleep in one room, which didn't work for long. We then stayed with my sister-in-law, Brenda, until we got our own temporary accommodations in Miami Lakes, courtesy of former Florida Governor Bob Graham, who was a senator at the time.

As the hurricane had caused an upheaval in our lives, so too was another type of storm that would rock our family. My daughter, Brasha Richardson, was born in 1992 as a result of an affair with a church member. Understandably, this rocked my family, and my wife contemplated divorce. She probably despised me at the time, but I've always loved her and never wanted to hurt her. After a time of separation, counseling, and much prayer, we were eventually reunited. Although I had my wife back, I knew things would never be quite the same. I would have to show her that she could trust me for, perhaps, the rest of my life. This was okay with me, because not having my family was like death. From that point, I didn't meet with women alone or entertain them for business purposes without my wife's presence. I put safeguards in place and asked God to uncover all hidden plots for temptation and seduction. Based on my experience, I would counsel up-and-coming ministers to beware of seductive spirits and seriously deal with any lusts within themselves. I told them to ensure their marriage and family were intact and thriving before trying to "save the world." I knew that if their home life wasn't in order, they could be led astray.

Shortly after conditions from Hurricane Andrew subsided, President George H. W. Bush assessed damage in the Miami area with Florida Governor Lawton Chiles. U.S. Representative Rev. Jesse Jackson also visited with politician Arthur Teele. The U.S. military was assigned to protect Perrine and dispense resources, like fresh water, to families. The storm caused an estimated $34 billion worth of damage and was identified as "the worst" natural disaster to occur in the United States prior to Hurricane Katrina. Janet Reno invited me to advise a group of business leaders on ways to help restore the businesses that were ruined and rebuild the buildings that had been destroyed in our area. She introduced me to Alvah Chapman, Jr., who had been the publisher of *The Miami Herald* and chairman of the Knight Ridder newspaper division, the second largest newspaper publisher in the United States until it was sold in 2006 (About: Chapman Partnership, 2021). He was like the godfather of Miami and was well connected in government. If he said anything about anything in Miami, it went that way. When he organized his group to tackle rebuilding efforts, it was all white Republicans. They were people who had been in conversations with the Bush adminis-tration. When President Bush asked what was needed, Alvah Chapman told him he needed to have a group, "We Will Rebuild," that could take care of whatever was going to be the shortfall of the estimated $34 billion of damage. So with Chapman's guidance, they organized a group to raise and distribute money throughout the community. Early on, they had identified some blacks who could be on the board, but there were no black people in the group in its initial phase, especially regarding religion. Sister Jeanne O'Laughlin, president of Barry University, was head of the religious committee, and she had very little connection to the black community. Her lack of association with the black religious community had nothing to do with anything negative about her; that just wasn't her realm. She was not anti-black community; she just didn't know anything about *us*. I served for a while as her cultural coach, so to speak. It was still difficult to get her to make a Kierkegaardian leap of faith from knowing nothing about the black community and religion to having her understand the implications of that community and become empowered to go forth.

I eventually became the chair of that committee and was able to leverage my authority to address the needs of the black community. Much of that was facilitated because of a meeting I had with Alvah Chapman and Janet Reno. Janet arranged this unforgettable meeting—she called me and said, "I want to bring Alvah Chapman down so he can see the black community. I want to see your church to get an idea of what goes on in Perrine, and you can help educate us." She brought Alvah Chapman down to my church, and there was no air conditioning, no lights. I was running my office with a generator.

They pulled up to the church in his brand-new Lexus. A wealthy, accomplished man, he preferred not to drive anything flashier. He purportedly only had two pair of shoes, a brown pair and a black pair, and didn't spend a lot of money on clothes. When he came to my office with Janet, he was wearing a business suit with a coat and tie. Janet noticed that the air conditioner was out, and she said, "Alvah, take off your damn jacket." He took it off and relaxed in his seat. He wanted the meeting to be a formal conversation, but she was intent upon everyone feeling comfortable and speaking freely. After our meeting, Alvah determined that I may be the best person to help with the mission of We Will Rebuild by helping to identify churches that did not have the funds to recover and those ministries and religious organizations that did not have insurance that could be used to rebuild. So, that became my civic role after the hurricane.

With a small committee, we were able to do a sweep of the South Dade Community and identify those churches that needed resources. We were able to allocate resources to most, if not all, of the damaged churches, most of them black. We also gave money to a synagogue in South Dade and to a Roman Catholic Church in Homestead that needed resources because they were underinsured. Several black churches got grants from the organization. The Reverend James C. Wise got funds for his church, Mount Pleasant Missionary Baptist Church, but this was somewhat controversial because his church was not on the original list of qualifying grant recipients. However, he was able to get a grant for approximately $119,000, one of the largest grants we gave. The average award was around $50,000, and it was invaluable assistance to the religious community that would have never happened unless the leadership of that committee had not changed. As part of the We Will Rebuild coalition of civic, business, and religious leaders, we raised $20 million for reconstruction and were authorized to allocate state money to businesses rebuilding after the hurricane. While serving as co-chair of the Religious Affairs Committee with Sis. Jeanne O'Laughlin, we were able to help hundreds of local businesses rebuild, as well as places of worship.

Our church builder, Harry Mursten, also served on the We Will Rebuild team. We had been in the new church, which his company built, for less than a year when Hurricane Andrew hit in 1992. The storm destroyed the church, leaving only the walls standing, and everything inside had been torn to shreds. I got a phone call one day shortly after the storm from Harry, who was calling to check on my family. When he asked about the church I said, "The church is destroyed."

He replied, "Well, as soon as we get operational, we will come and dry the church." Continuing, he asked if the roof was still intact.

"No, the roof is not intact."

"Well, the first thing we got to do is put the roof back."

As promised, his construction crew came out to the church and removed all the moisture. Next, they began on the roof. By July 1993, the church was fully reconstructed and reconfigured to some degree. The church's insurance paid for everything, including the Mursten company's $38,000 in expenses, which covered the cost of materials and labor. Harry Mursten refused to take any money for his company's work, though. He knew the church resided in an economically depressed community and wanted to help.

I checked the church mailbox one day, and to my surprise, there was a letter from Mursten Construction. Harry Mursten sent the church a letter and check for $38,000, explaining that he didn't want to accept anything for the work. Not only did he give the money back, he also donated a Hammond Organ that he had at his church. Himself a classical pianist, he said no one even knew how to use the organ. "We got it here, and we're not using it," he said.

This was quite a timely, significant gift since the church's Hammond Organ had been destroyed in the storm. The organ that Sweet Home has to this day came from Harry Mursten and his church, which is in Miami Lakes. He died in August 2016, and I cried because he was such a good man.

While getting our church and other churches rebuilt and restored was quite a feat, my focus remained steadfast on the community as a whole, especially in Homestead, where the storm had nearly obliterated homes, businesses, and its most significant economic infrastructure: a military base. My work with We Will Rebuild granted me access to work with local dignitaries but restoring Homestead would require federal input at the highest levels. Miraculously, I was able to express my concerns to the President of the United States himself.

During a televised town hall meeting with newly elected President Bill Clinton on February 10, 1993, which was moderated locally by newswoman Ann Bishop of WPLG-Channel 10, Clinton inquired about what Miami needed after Hurricane Andrew's devastation. Local community leaders, including myself, were asked to be a part of this town hall panel, during which we got a chance to ask the president direct questions.

After Ann Bishop introduced President Clinton, I was given the opportunity to ask the first question. I asked about the recovery of Homestead Air Force Base, because we had lost a lot of people and jobs, and it had detrimental impact on the economic condition of the surrounding area. On September 3, 1992, as a Democratic presidential nominee, Clinton had visited Lauren Roberts Park, at what used to be Homestead Air Force Base. He had pledged to rebuild the Air Force base and to have the federal government pay for all the repairs to public facilities struck down by Hurricane Andrew (Anderson 1993).

Clinton answered it diplomatically, promising to rebuild or replace the base with *"something else...to generate an equal number of jobs"* (Clark and Yanez 1993). When he came to Miami to address some of the concerns that were raised in a town hall meeting, I was given the opportunity to meet him face to face and to talk to him. I took a picture with him during our first in-person meeting. I got a chance to see him several times after that during his presidency.

I continued to make connections I knew would benefit the less fortunate and disenfranchised in Miami-Dade County, namely the South Dade area. One such occasion was working as an advisor to Alvah Chapman on the Homeless Trust. He flew me and a couple of other community leaders to Orlando to see that city's version of a homeless assistance program. Before Alvah embarked on what he was going to do in our area, he wanted all of us community stakeholders at that time to see how it had worked in Orlando. In 1995, Chapman Partnership, in fact, opened Miami-Dade County's first Homeless Assistance Center in downtown Miami. Three years later, in 1998, the Partnership opened a second such center in Homestead (About: Chapman Partnership 2021).

25

PASTOR'S STUDY

One of my gifts as it relates to preaching is to take the Bible and have it make sense for current times. I think the Bible always needs to be contemporized, and for the ministry that does not do that, I think it is doing a great disservice to our community. If a pastor just preached a story that Mary had a little lamb and it has no application to what's going on right now, then the members must and will discover important social themes elsewhere. What they get from another source, outside the church, may not complement scriptural teachings or a biblical approach, so a conscientious ministry should seek to usher members through today's world using the scripture. Thus, the message in the black church, for instance, should relate to political challenges that we have—social justice issues, and police brutality. Mary had a little lamb should essentially come alive for the 21st century.

Rev. Ferguson, I think, put me on edge with this notion. In the Pentecostal church, we didn't have that kind of contemporary focus. Our aim then was to get everybody saved so they could go to heaven. We were always looking at otherworldliness, beyond what's happening now, because we have absolutely no control over what's happening now. That was the attitude and perhaps even the philosophy of what was presented from the Pentecostal pulpit. When I became a part of the ministry at Second Baptist, Rev. Ferguson always talked about the need for black ministers to do the best they could in their context, to make things better for everybody, taking the Bible and having it make sense. His prime objective with me was to make sure every black man had education. He felt there was no excuse for not having an education, and he influenced me to continue pursuing my education, not just for a title, but to better lead my community.

By 1989, I had begun my doctoral program, but it did not work for me for many reasons, including Hurricane Andrew, irreconcilable philosophical differences with some professors, inability to tailor my program to introduce religious and social themes, and my inability to grasp and remember some of the great foundational teachings in philosophy. Furthermore, I felt the information, training, and education I was receiving had no correlation to my work as a Baptist preacher. I was being trained to teach philosophy, not preach the gospel or heal the social ills of my community. So, after completing most of the coursework for the program, I did not return.

I then pursued a more practical academic program for ministry, which I discovered while reading a pastoral journal. The program was located in Newburgh, Indiana, and only required occasional trips there for major tests and the like. After I applied and was accepted, I transferred some of my credits from the University of Miami. I completed my coursework in Pastoral Counseling and my dissertation after three years. I then defended my dissertation in October 1995 and was subsequently awarded a Doctor of Philosophy degree in Biblical Counseling. While I was studying, I was also teaching at St. Thomas University in the School of Religion and History, as I had been since January 1990. I taught the Introduction to Religion at both campuses until 2015.

While I navigated through and worked in higher education, I noticed an unsettling employment trend: the lack of people who looked like me in upper management. I knew this was something I wanted to change when I got the opportunity, and that chance did come while I concluded my doctoral program. I have served on several boards wherein I was one of two or the only person of color. When I served as a board of trustees member for Miami Dade College, my goal, as one of two blacks, was to ensure that qualified people of color could get opportunities for advancement in higher education. As a result, I had some tremendous arguments with the outgoing president, Dr. Robert McCabe, at that time over this issue. The new president, Eduardo Padron, was sensitive to issues of diversity and inclusion, but he would not promote black males. He only promoted black females because he could "kill two birds with one stone," as they say. He could effectively satisfy both gender and racial inequalities by simply hiring or promoting a black woman. He wouldn't then need to hire a black man because he could defend his detractors about not hiring enough minorities.

As a black man, I was obviously offended at the notion of eliminating possibilities for the advancement of black men. The entire time I served on the board, we could never agree on that, and that's probably one of my biggest disappointments. To this day, there are no prominent black males in the Miami Dade College system. Not one. There are no black male deans or executives in top administrative positions.

I've been allowed and invited to participate in many instances wherein I was the only or first black person. I have never taken these opportunities lightly in terms of my civic responsibility because, at one point, I was considered the religious voice for the South Dade area. Remembering the lessons my mother taught about the way I needed to present myself, I always tried to speak with clear diction and direction. Because of my pluralistic worldview, I have been able to discuss social challenges with an optimism that has generated concrete solutions and resources. As a pastor, I try to make those who are not part of black culture understand our particular context when it comes down to identifying challenges. While helping others understand and facilitate the needs of the black community, I've also had to recognize some harmful patterns in the church community.

The black church has undergone many attacks, and one of the most recognized has been prosperity preaching. However, another one involves the pride and arrogance of African-American pastors through the use of titles such as bishop, archbishop and doctor. Unfortunately, people in many of our churches don't understand the difference between a DD and a PhD. All they know is they get a chance to call their pastor "doctor."

I was playing golf one day with a group of ministers, and a theological question came up. One guy said, "Walter, what do you think about this?" Before I could get a chance to respond, another gentleman responded, giving his opinion, which by the way, was wrong. I simply listened and made no further attempt to comment about the subject.

Noticing my silence, another man urged, "What do you think about that?"

I said, "We'll discuss this later if you're really serious about it."

"You think you're so damn smart," he balked.

"I don't think I'm that smart," I responded. "I just I think I have a different set of experiences, you know. We all do. We all have different experiences."

"You think because they call you 'doctor' it makes you smarter, but I got a doctorate just like you, by the way."

He had an honorary doctorate from a school in which all you have to do is pay a few hundred dollars, and they give you a diploma that reads DD, or Doctor of Divinity. There is no formal degree in academia called Doctor of Divinity. So, to get a DD, you're not going to school, doing research, or writing a paper. Instead, you're presented with an opportunity to apply for it because of your contribution to society or your community. No one in the church is going to take the time to investigate where or how a pastor gets his or her "doctor" designation.

The same is true of the term "bishop" and the like. In 1993, I took a minister who called himself "bishop" with me to a We Will Rebuild meeting shortly after Hurricane Andrew. We were in the midst of several guys who were legitimate denominational leaders, such as Archbishop Edward McCarthy of the Roman Catholic Archdiocese of Miami. He saw me and said, "Hello, Walter."

I responded, as I always had, using his official title, "Hello, Archbishop."

"How are you doing, Walter? How did you make out after the storm?"

"I'm okay, and so is my family," I explained. "But as you may know, we lost use of the church, and I lost my home."

"Walter, that is so unfortunate. How are you doing now?"

"Well, we've recovered. The church is under repair, and we are going to be okay."

"So, who's that with you?"

"This is my friend…"

"Bishop Wheeler," my friend interrupted.

"Hi, bishop. It's good to meet you. If you're a friend of Walter, then you're a friend of mine."

"Yes, sir. Yes, sir," my friend beamed proudly.

"By the way, where is your jurisdiction?" continued Archbishop McCarthy.

Bishop Wheeler looked at me as if to say, '*What's a jurisdiction?*'

"What [churches] are you in charge of?"

He clearly had no idea of what to say, and so Archbishop McCarthy just left it alone. My friend had made himself a bishop because that was a popular title to have in the ministry at that time. Bishop is typically part of an episcopacy, a hierarchical form of church government. Episcopalians have no one central church leader, so there's always somebody above the pastor. So there's the pastor, somebody who's above the pastor, and then somebody above that, which consists of three hierarchical layers. This is not the structure of most Christian churches in America. My friend was the pastor of a church, and he had one location with fewer than 20 members. Nevertheless, he called himself "bishop," which is unheard of in the Roman Catholic Church or in any Episcopalian church government. The black church went through this self-appointed title phase for quite a while.

The title "reverend" has to do with the fact that you are ordained, so anyone who has not been through an ordination process should not be called reverend. In the religious community, you are respected because you have been ordained and recognized by your denomination after having gone through a process to become a professional pastor or professional leader in a spiritual context. Some people start churches and preaching, so they start calling themselves "reverend." However, that's not right because the title reverend always implies ordination. I personally don't like using both titles in front of my name: Reverend Doctor or vice versa. I prefer to go by Rev. Walter T. Richardson, Ph.D.

The black church's leadership has gone through several vanity title phases. For instance, pastors were called "reverend" even though some of them had not been ordained. That was considered a high-ranking title back in the day. Then we got to a point where people wanted to be called "doctor" who hadn't even gone to college or even finished high school. Now, there's a new title that's in vogue. It's the title of "bishop," which sounds so authoritative and spiritual. People have really jumped at the opportunity of being consecrated as a bishop. At one point, I was excited about the possibility, but it didn't resonate with me enough to allow confusion in my congregation. Beyond bishop, when people call themself an "apostle," that puts them way ahead of everybody else, because it refers to those who were directly commissioned or appointed by Christ to preach the full gospel.

There was a big meeting of Baptist pastors in Pensacola, Florida, in 1992, and Paul S. Morton, Sr. was invited to preach. His dynamic, animated presentation style was effective in getting and maintaining attention, so we all looked forward to it. On the night that he preached, all the younger pastors went out to dinner together. Most of us were in our 30s and 40s at the time. During dinner, Paul introduced the idea of having a group of pastors who would be a bit more progressive than the National Baptist Convention. He had been in charge of the late-night services during the convention, when all the preachers came together to have a midnight service with other dynamic preachers and talented singers joining the service. This provided some spunk in the convention, which was run by elder preachers. He and his family, as well as others, knew that we would probably never ascend to leadership in the National Baptist Convention because we were considered "young." You had to be old to even qualify for leadership consideration, so Paul thought it would be a good idea to have a separate movement of young pastors who had several things in common. Number one, they were not anti-women in ministry. Number two, they were not anti-movement of the Spirit in the church, where it was okay to sing, shout, and use instruments other than an organ or piano during praise. Number three, they were not against divine healing by laying on of hands or the use of anointing oil.

He espoused what is called the "Full Gospel" movement, which is associated with Pentecostalism. It refers to when Paul said, "...I have fully preached the gospel of Christ" (Romans 15:19 NKJV). A Full Gospel Christian believes that the Holy Spirit is still operating today as He did in the New Testament, namely in the book of Acts. The Spirit is still healing, giving spiritual gifts, performing miracles, and so forth. Paul wanted to find other Baptist pastors who embraced this kind of theology. I was all for it, as was Carlos Malone, who was in the initial meeting along with Walter O'Shea Granger. Once we got back home, we all constantly spoke with Paul about how we should proceed. Eventually, we started meeting with other pastors around the country who were also interested in starting this neo-Charismatic Baptist movement. Originally, it was going to be called the "Full Gospel Fellowship of Pastors." It was going to comprise pastors who had similar philosophies and understanding of what church could be, but we would maintain our Baptist membership and affiliation. We would meet regularly, but we had not worked out all the details of how and when to execute this vision. Still, we knew we wanted to be united because we had so much in common in terms of our religious backgrounds. Paul Morton's father was a leader in the Church of God in Christ in Canada and Detroit, and my dad was a bishop in the Pentecostal church. Other group members also had Pentecostal relatives, or they themselves had been reared in the Pentecostal church. As such, there was never any question among us about the legitimacy of women in ministry, the use of tambourines, drums and other less common instruments, shouting in the

Spirit, or speaking in tongues. In the initial structure, we agreed on the senior pastor's title being "bishop" because that's biblical. We would not use terms like "president" or "moderator," as these were not biblical. Certainly, "bishop" was commonplace to Paul with his dad already being a bishop. Similarly, my great uncle who founded our church was called bishop, so I was behind that decision. Paul was going to be the bishop, and we would be "pastors" because he believed that every pastor needs a pastor. All of us were going to embrace this structure, and we kind of knew intuitively that because it was his vision, he would be the bishop. He was a young, energetic, compelling speaker, but not as well-trained as some of the people with whom he eventually aligned himself. This didn't matter—he was trained enough to provide spiritual leadership. Thus, he became the obvious choice to be the bishop of this organization of pastors.

As the group developed, he decided to follow the model of bishop within some of the other Pentecostal organizations and Methodist churches, which are Episcopal in nature, meaning headed by a bishop and having a hierarchical structure. His idea was to have 12 bishops, with him being the senior bishop. Under him would be other bishops that would help run the organization. This is when we also got information about perhaps bringing our churches under this hierarchy. At this point, I pushed back a little because I wanted to know from where these bishops would come. Paul explained, saying, "They will come from people like you all who are on the phone with me. You would be in charge of certain activities."

Carlos Malone was chosen to be the executive secretary, so he would be somewhat like the "Bishop of Administration." Kenneth Ulmer was identified for this team, and he was going to be the assistant to the senior bishop, providing oversight. I was going to be the bishop in charge of music and worship. As they were developing this plan, I started seeing some holes in it, and every time I would mention one of the holes, I got pushback from those who were really gung-ho about doing this. I pointed out, "If we're calling ourselves Baptists, how does this set with the larger organization from which we're trying to separate ourselves? If we're really pastors and we're going to be supported by a bishop, there's got to be some necessary overlap with what our churches are doing and how they perceive us."

They kind of talked their way through that, which was still unacceptable to me, but then I asked the question that ultimately broke my relationship

Walter T. Richardson   155

with the group. I asked, "If anything happens to one of us, as part of this fellowship of pastors, and we leave our congregation, what happens with the pastor who succeeds us? Will he be named or chosen by this group or the bishop? Or, will the church be autonomous, as they've always been in the Baptist circles, and select their own pastor?"

Those questions never really got answered. The few answers that were proffered were not satisfactory to me. As such, I chose not to be a part of that organization. I stopped going to the meetings even though I had all the paperwork, and I was going to be perhaps even made a bishop. I said, "Listen, this is too loosely organized. We've not sufficiently thought this through. I wish you the best, but I don't think I can be a part of this and at the same time have the influence with my congregation without them being suspicious of my motives." That's when I parted ways with that organization.

My resignation brought about some challenges. Bishop Malone, who is over Bethel Baptist Church in Richmond Heights, and I were once very close. As a result of me bowing out of the Full Gospel Fellowship of Pastors, our relationship became a little fractured. It was the same with everyone else, all the other guys who were my ministry friends. Even Victor Curry, one of my best friends, who was going to be the "bishop of stewardship." He had a problem with me and actually aired his frustration with my decision on AM 1490 WMBM radio station, which he owned. The organization went on to be officially called "The Full Gospel Baptist Church Fellowship International," and it has become one of the largest African-American church organizations in the country with hundreds of affiliated churches. After Bishop Paul Morton stepped down in 2015, Bishop Joseph W. Walker III became the presiding bishop.

26

SAYING GOOD-BYE
TO MOTHER

The last time I saw my mother alive was Thursday, October 10, 1996. She was in the hospice unit of North Shore Hospital and was being given increasingly stronger doses of morphine for pain. My brother had come down from Georgia with his wife, Corliss, and my wife, daughter, and her six-month-old son, Tyler, were in the room. My mother smiled and recognized her second grandchild and played with the baby as he sat on her hospital bed. She called him "Mr. President," in a sense blessing him. I knew her time left here on earth was short, so we soaked up every moment to hear her talk, sing, and share stories. None of us had recording devices, and cell phones with recording features did not exist then. None of us thought to bring cameras, even though we knew these were the last and treasured moments with our beloved.

I left the next day on a flight to St. Thomas, Virgin Islands, to preach and conduct a music workshop for Pastor Bentley Thomas. I truly believed my mother, although very sick, had a few more days left. I was scheduled to return to the United States on Sunday afternoon.

I conducted the music workshop Friday evening and Saturday during the day, and Pastor Thomas took me to a wonderful restaurant following the workshop. The seafood was exquisite, and I enjoyed lobster and other delicacies. He dropped me off at my hotel around 7:30 p.m. so I could prepare to preach the next morning. When I got to my room, the message light on my phone was blinking. No one in St. Thomas knew where I was staying other than the pastor and since he had just dropped me off, I was curious about the blinking light. I tried to call downstairs but no one answered. So, I walked downstairs to the lobby only to determine that no one was working at that time of night. Something inside of me said, "Try to reach home and pay the charges when you check out." So, I managed to dial the U.S. to my house and again, no one answered. So, I tried to call my mother's house. One of my relatives from out of town was visiting and answered the phone. They gave the phone to my father, who sounded upbeat and asked how I was doing since I was out of the country. I told him I was fine, but had not been able to reach Dolores, my wife. He said, "Hold on, she's here."

Before he gave her the phone, I asked about my mom. I said, "Daddy, how's Momma doing?"

He answered quickly and said, "Son, I thought you knew, and that's why you were calling. Your mother passed away!"

I cannot describe my response when I heard that. I was angry and surprised, too composed to scream outwardly, but mostly confused. Several thoughts ran concurrently through my mind while I tried to gather myself to continue the conversation. I asked one more question, "When did this happen?"

My father said, "Just a while ago around six something!"

My wife then came to the phone and told me how sad she was for me, not being able to be there in Miami, and that the family was looking forward to my return Sunday afternoon. There were no flights leaving St. Thomas that evening, and the flight that I had scheduled for return to Miami was the earliest flight I could take. So after speaking with Dolores and hanging up the hotel phone, in an empty hotel silent except for the waves pushing against the shore outside my room, I fell to my knees. Before I opened my mouth to talk to the Lord, a verse of scripture came to mind, "This is the day that the Lord has made." It was a strange meditational response to such a tragic moment in my life, but I was being urged by the Spirit to rejoice and be glad.

I don't remember crying, but I do remember smiling and reminiscing, and wishing I could be home with relatives and friends. I called Pastor Thomas and told him what happened. He prayed with me and asked if I wanted to be relieved of preaching and leading the music ministry for Sunday, and I told him I would, with the help of the Lord, do the job I was requested to do.

I preached the next day at Bethel Church, and I worshipped with the choir that I had trained the previous days. I did not announce the death of my mother until the service had ended. I only mentioned it then because I did not want to mingle in fellowship following the services. I wanted to be alone at the airport and wait for my flight home.

My flight had a layover in Puerto Rico, but I reached the Miami International Airport later that day, October 13th, and when I went to retrieve my luggage, I was met by several deacons from Sweet Home. Deacon Simmons, Deacon Ivery, and Deacon Ganzy came to pick me up and take care of me, their pastor. I don't remember anything that was said in the car on the way to my father's house. The 20-minute ride from the airport to our destination seemed to take an eternity. Once we arrived, the deacons gently transferred me and my belongings to my people. They made sure I had everything I needed and left. These men never knew how the gesture of them caring for me in my most vulnerable hour positively impacted me and further jelled our pastor-deacons relationship. After some time spent with the family at my dad's house, Dolores and I left for our home, intending to return the next morning.

I met my dad and brother Monday morning, and I felt the need to explode. It was similar to the feeling people get when they know they have to vomit. I went to my mom's bedroom, the room that I actually occupied as a teenager, and stood at the door. My mom, months earlier, had placed a lock on the door, so my dad had to let me in. While he was getting the key to the room, I started shouting, "Momma, Momma!" over and over again. As I shouted, I pounded the door with my palms harder and harder. Had I used my balled up fist, I would have broken the door or my hands. In my confused state, I was sober enough to not cause irreparable injury to my hands, as my mother taught me to always protect my hands as a pianist. My father had the key, but did not come to the door, and would not let anyone else come to help me. I could sense others wanted to see about me, but he told them to let me "get it out." Once I stopped screaming and pounding, he came and opened the door. I looked in her room, but could not go in. I closed the door and quickly joined my family in the living room and sat there with everyone in total silence. No one had ever seen me react this way, and I don't remember ever reacting that way to anything.

That year also memorialized the end of our church's fiduciary obligation to the loan we took out to finance the new church building in 1991. Galvanized by our efforts to rebuild and resume without debt, the congregation was able to pay off the church mortgage in four years. By 1996, we owed nothing more to lenders and decided to host a symbolic "mortgage burning." To my knowledge, no other large organization, especially a church, had been able to settle their mortgage in such as short window of time.

I invited New Mount Olive Baptist Church from Fort Lauderdale to come and be part of that commemorative service on a Sunday afternoon. The ministry was led by the renowned Dr. Mack King Carter, who was my good friend, and he and his congregation were among those who were on hand to witness the burning of our mortgage. We took a copy of the mortgage, and literally set it aflame. I had the oldest member of the church, who at that time was a lady named Edna Collin, burn the first page of the mortgage. She and her husband were two of the founders of our church. I then had the youngest member, my godson, Gentle Hamilton III, burn the last page of the mortgage. Edna literally burned the first page in a big stainless steel bowl, representing the first members of the church. Then Gentle came along, representing the last member under the mortgage, to ignite the last page.

27

BIG HONORS

I had earned a bachelor's and master's degree from St. Thomas by 1989, and I began teaching full time at St. Thomas University during the spring semester of 1990. After I had mentored other students while I was a student, Dr. Joe and Mercedes Iannone thought I'd be a welcome addition to their staff, but one of the most significant factors in their decision was the fact that I am black. There were no blacks teaching in the religion department and a large percentage of the students at St. Thomas were members of the black diaspora from the Caribbean countries and the Americas.

The chair of the religion department, Dr. Olga Hutchinson, sat through one of my classes early into the semester. She commented to me that she had never experienced that much excitement between a teacher and the students in a classroom. From that point, she would occasionally speak to me about teaching paradigms and come to visit my class sessions with regularity. Soon other students were auditing my class. Dr. Hutchinson ultimately learned of my community involvement and my views about social justice, and without saying a word to me, she recommended me for an honorary doctorate in 1997.

The following year, 1998, was a big year for me. The church was doing well with tremendous membership increases, finances, and community involvement. However, I was working long, crazy hours. I would go to the church right after breakfast and stay until the evening, rarely taking time to eat lunch. I neither took days off nor vacationed. As an official employee and head of the church, I didn't even have codified requirements about sick days, days off, and vacations. I watched my father ensure that we always went on family vacations, mainly to North Carolina, but taking time off just wasn't important to me.

I released my first book, "Going through Samaria," in 1999. It was a condensation of my dissertation, which I had been working on throughout graduate school. It provided the inspiration for this book on the woman of Samaria from the Gospel of John 4:4-26, where the apostle talked about how Jesus and this woman were so different—culturally, religiously, and otherwise. Yet, Jesus was effective in getting her to see life from another perspective, and as a result changed the woman's life forever. Since my academic concentration was on pastoral counseling, I thought this biblical account provided a good example of how people can be changed by others, even if they don't necessarily look like them or act like them. Thus, Jesus became the model that needs to be followed as it relates to counseling. The complete title of my dissertation was "The Impact of Cultural Diversity and Biblical Counseling." Similarly, my mission was to transform people's lives through my interactions in the community.

No one ever tells you that when you take on civic roles for the cause of community revival or social justice that you may become a victim, being targeted by the bad guys and even the good guys who are invested in maintaining the status quo. Sometimes activists get threatened verbally and physically on the very streets they're trying to reform. We may get arrested for breaking unfamiliar laws about gathering and marching in particular places or at particular times. Meanwhile, there are those who get pulled into the very lawlessness they're trying to combat, such as prostitution and drug use, but their heart's desire is to help. There are certainly liabilities, and costs attached to success of any kind. My civic success almost cost me my family at one point. My time and attention were disproportionately focused on the church and its community involvement rather than my family.

My family, many times, was put on the back burner because there was no way I could spend most of my time doing community work and still maintain adequate time with family. I lost sight of my priorities. I almost lost my son Walter because I didn't spend enough time with him in my formative years as a pastor. What's more painful is that I almost lost my daughter, who truly needed my loving reinforcement and wisdom in choosing a mate, along with other significant young adult decisions. Because they didn't see their daddy enough, they were making life choices counter to my desire (or even awareness) to some degree. Something had to give. My wife, who had been very patient with me, recognized this when I turned 50. She had conversations with members of Shepherd's Care Ministry about suggesting activities I would enjoy that would take me away from the busy life of pastoring so I could relax and enjoy life away from the pulpit.

She spoke with Shepherd's president, Barbara Grace, explaining, "I gotta find something for my husband to do to get him out of the office. He's working seven days a week, and I'm losing my husband. He loves his work. He loves what he's done in the community, but there's got to be something else he can do to get him out of the office to spend time with his family."

Barbara says, "I got it." With the guidance of my fraternity brother George, she figured I needed a distraction and found the perfect one: golf.

The Sunday before my birthday, the church held a surprise gathering at Holy Rosary Catholic Church social hall. My wife fooled me and told me something else was going on there, but when I arrived, the place was filled with familiar faces from Sweet Home and then I knew something strange and wonderful was going on. I received many gifts and many encouraging words were spoken, but then Barbara called me up for a final presentation. It was an envelope. I opened the envelope in front of everyone expecting a monetary gift. Instead, it was a gift certificate for golf lessons. I publicly showed delight, but inwardly, I was stunned. I had not mentioned to anyone that I even liked golf. As a matter of fact, I didn't. I never saw the sense in hitting a tiny ball, and then trying to locate it to hit it again. Still, I graciously accepted my final gift. After the event was over, Barbara explained that George had made arrangements with a golf pro to teach me how to play and I was to begin the next day, which would force me to take my day off.

They had paid for a golf pro to start my golf lessons on Monday, so it seemed that I didn't have much choice. "You can't go to work," announced Barbara. "You have to go take your golf lessons. You just gotta show up."

I called the golf pro, Joe "Roach" Delancy, later that day, and after a few short words of instruction, he told me to meet him Monday morning around 11 at the Biltmore Hotel golf course.

As instructed, I went to the hotel and met this 83-year-old man who was there to teach me the game of golf. He was carrying an old golf bag with some old golf clubs filled with old golf balls. He showed me how to hold each club using several different "grips," and told me how to stand, and for the rest of that hour, I never hit a golf ball.

He asked me to return the next day at the same time, which I did. I went after 3 p.m. the next few days, but for the first week, I spent every day, including Sunday afternoon, with Joe Roach. When I was not swinging the club or when I was taking a break, Joe would tell me how he got involved in golf. He was from Coconut Grove, the son of immigrant parents from the Bahamas. After school, he and several other boys would make money caddying for rich white men who played golf. He said the white men would let them play with their 7-irons after the day was over, and the black boys would practice and play using that one club to drive, chip, and putt.

That was more than 20 years ago, and I've not stopped playing golf since. I have also started spending a ton more time with my family and friends and doing other things that I like to do in addition to ministry, including travel. I took a trip to Israel in 2000 for the 2,000th anniversary of the Lord's birth as part of a coalition of religious leaders from the United States. I was selected to be on that trip among a diverse group of believers, including Protestant Christians, Roman Catholic Christians, and Jews. Three bishops accompanied us, and we all understood the potential dangers, as protests and violence had followed a series of attempted peace accords and treaties focused on solutions on Jerusalem, the West Bank, and other contested areas.

This trip was not just significant for me, but also for my congregation back home. It tied it in to help me kind of put some definition and clarity to some of the people, places and things that are mentioned in the scriptures and to retrace the steps of Jesus. I was better able to understand the Palestinians and Muslims and what they meant to the Holy Land because it's the founding home of the three major religions. All the Abrahamic religions were founded right there in Jerusalem. The Jews are there, the Muslims are there, and the Christians are there. As such, there is quite a bit of interaction between these three groups, and who has the right to be there. In many instances, while we were touring and having conversation with community leaders, they were quite clear that at most of the sites there was ample due respect to all the religious traditions to allow them access at certain times. For example, when I went to the place that is purportedly the birthplace of Jesus, the Christian churches had places where they could worship. Then there were places like the River Jordan, where Jews had some spiritual and historical significance in Hebrew Scripture. Essentially, there were sites where the Jews would worship separate from Christians and Muslims and vice versa. We witnessed a lot of respect there, and we came to know in what areas the lines were blurry and those where the line was clear, restricting access to a particular group. The Wailing Wall, for instance, was a daily worship place exclusively for the Jews that were in old Jerusalem. Once I got back to Sweet Home after my one-week visit, I did a full slide presentation for the congregation, which was packed. I shared as much as I could about the customs and culture I had witnessed.

I feel part of my calling and responsibility is to adequately educate those under my tutelage and ministerial influence about religion's impact on racial, cultural, and even political dynamics, and vice versa. Many of my students wanted to know more about Islam when I was teaching world religion at St. Thomas University. Prior to the attack on the World Trade Towers on September 11, 2001, I systematically covered all the seven major religions, but a major portion of my presentation focused on Islam. After 9/11, however, I chose to focus on only the five religious traditions, including Islam, Christianity, Judaism, Hinduism, and Buddhism. Again, I put a lot of emphasis on Islam, but this time, it was somewhat different. A lot of articles, books, and broadcasts were spewing misinformation, so I had to explain the difference in mindsets within the same religion, from radical extremists to loving adherents. I discussed how some people can become radicalized, and how the basic foundations of these religions are absolutely pure. Well-intended or well-informed people who had an interaction with God seek to honor Him, but somewhere along the line, somebody missed the core message and took it off track. And that's what happened with the radicalization of Christianity, Islam, and Judaism. I have taught about all of this.

During that time, I even hosted a Bible study series at the church that delved into religious radicalization. As a result, church members reached out to people who they knew were Muslims and brought them to Sweet Home. In fact, an Imam came and sat near the back of the church. After the service, he told me he was impressed that a Christian knew so much about Islam and was willing to share it with others.

What he didn't know was that this type of exposure was part of my preaching philosophy, so to speak. Some religious leaders feel that if they restrict their following's knowledge to only what the leader feels is important or necessary, the members will be more restrained and dedicated. I, however, feel quite the opposite. I have always explained to the members that, as Christians, everybody doesn't worship the same way, and that's fine. When I got to Sweet Home initially, this approach was met with some resistance that I hadn't encountered at Second Baptist. At Sweet Home, other ministers were resistant to allow me to be a part of their inner circle because I had a Pentecostal background. They were afraid I would start speaking in tongues, introducing tambourines and encourage unbridled worship, all things Pentecostal. They were genuinely afraid of this, and some expressed it to mutual pastor friends, who would come back and tell me. I don't know whether that was intentional, knowing they would share it with me, but no one ever said anything to my face. Nevertheless, I spent a lot of time educating my people about the diversity of religious expression and attitudes within Christianity. I spoke about Pentecostals, Presbyterians, Episcopalians, and Catholics. I've spent a lot of time talking about the difference between Catholicism and Protestantism because they needed to understand and never make the mistake of generalizing and becoming misled.

28

THE GOSPEL IN BLACK
AND WHITE

I was a young boy when I became fully aware of the fact that even though we're all serving the same God, we worship differently and respect race differently. I remember going with my dad and Great Aunt Mamie, who took over as pastor of the church after her husband died, to a Church of God of Prophecy convention that was completely filled with black parishioners parading around the church with banners, representing the places where they come from around the country. In the pulpit sat one lone white man. I asked specifically, "What's his role?"

Turns out that he was supervisor of the service. "What does that mean?" I inquired further. They couldn't have conventions without the presence of a white supervisor. Blacks weren't even left to their own devices in worshipping God. They had to have a white person there as a superintendent to make sure everything was in order.

My determination, after years in ministry, is that blacks and whites in America have a different view of the same God. I've been criticized because most of my prayers for the last several years have ended with me saying, "We pray this prayer in the name of the Negro from Nazareth named Jesus." I say this as I close my prayers, and I don't care where I am.

When you visit Sweet Home Missionary Baptist Church, the stained-glass windows feature a picture of a black Jesus, not a European-looking man. There is no depiction of Jesus with fair skin, blue eyes and a straight nose, as has commonly been featured in Christian artwork and graphics. In fact, I drew the depiction of Jesus in the Jordan River being baptized by his cousin John. I drew Jesus' face after, I felt, the artist we hired couldn't get it right. We commissioned the artwork to a local artist who we felt could capture a more accurate rendition of Jesus as a black man. We requested that the stained-glass window company make sure that all the figures in the scene I wanted to show were properly adapted based on my description. I wanted to show Jesus being baptized in a traditional scene, but I also wanted to show diversity in that scene. I wanted a woman in that scene. I wanted a child in that scene. In general, I wanted to show that Jesus was available to His community of believers who comprised not just men, but also women and children of various backgrounds.

So very prominent in a picture at Sweet Home is a woman who's standing by watching Jesus get baptized. Featured prominently in that picture is also a little boy who has across his shoulder five fish and two loaves of bread, a reference to Jesus miraculously feeding the multitudes. However, I didn't draw him. Neither did I draw the woman nor John the Baptist either.

When I got the rendition from the artist of what Jesus was supposed to look like, I didn't like it. So, I called the company and said, "Listen, this looks good. It's almost perfect, and I think you got the idea. I love everything about this picture, but Jesus doesn't look the way I think he should look."

The company rep replied, "Well, this artwork was done by a Haitian artist. He knows what he's doing, but we could have him do it over."

I said, "Okay. Again, the woman looks fine. The boy looks fine. John the Baptist looks fine. He's got dreadlocks. He looks fine. But Jesus does not look the way I think he needs to be represented at Sweet Home Baptist Church. Have him do it over."

This man took great pain in doing it again and again. He tried two more times. Finally, I said to my members, "I'm going to give this a stab myself. I'm going to try this. I'm going to draw this image, but I haven't drawn in a while. I need to give them an idea of what Jesus ought to look like, and I'm going to make it as good as I can, so that if possible, it might get adopted in some form. If it's good enough, they can adapt it and maybe just superimpose what I've done into the picture. Just cut and paste."

They didn't have a problem with that. As it turned out, the artist, the Haitian gentleman who was originally doing it, thought my work was much better than his work. He implored them to go ahead and use it, so my rendition is what's up at Sweet Home right now.

In the Key of M

The window art that we did for the former church building, before we moved, was done by an artist who was sensitive to that. He depicted Jesus the right way, as a black man. *The Miami Herald* newspaper did a big story on me and the depiction of black Jesus. The article featured two local churches, including Sweet Home. The other church was New Hope Baptist Church in Liberty City, where the pastor's name is Randall Holts. That church had a window that also featured Jesus as a black man, which inspired me to make sure that what I did at Sweet Home represented Jesus in His blackness. So, I have no problem talking about Jesus as a black man, particularly because it is declared in Scripture. Revelation chapter one talks about Jesus as the Alpha and Omega. John, the author, says he sees Jesus, and he's got burned feet, wooly hair, and bloodshot eyes. That said, I have no problem with my artwork or prayer. If white folks ever figured out that Jesus was black, they would probably leave Christianity.

The black church provides its members with an opportunity to learn of their equal identity, role, and responsibility in carrying out the call of Christ, but its reason for being in existence has not been satisfied. Until 1845, for the most part, there was no need for a "black church." We just had the church, but because of racism and people being overlooked, it necessitated having a black church. For instance, the AME, or African Methodist Episcopal Church, came about in 1787 because Methodists forced black members to sit in a separate area, which was called "the bigger Heaven" located in the balcony (Dickerson 2016). Richard Allen felt the need to pray, so he went down to the altar, which was the custom of people who wanted to pray before services. The white members accosted him and told him he couldn't pray down there because he did not belong there. So, they took that as a point of departure and left to organize the African Methodist Episcopal Church and what later became known as the African Methodist Episcopal Zion Church. A former slave, Allen built the Bethel African Methodist Church in Philadelphia and successfully sued the Pennsylvania courts to gain independence from white Methodists in 1815. Because of slavery, black people wanted to be part of the church and worship experience to which they had been introduced. Religion was in their DNA, as they came from Africa as religious people. In 1845, they were told that blacks and whites couldn't worship together, so the Southern Baptist Church pulled away from what was then called the American Baptist Church. Even in spirituality, whites didn't see blacks as their equals, so they were not going to worship with them. That's how the movement of black churches, black Baptist churches in particular, came about. They didn't think blacks were human enough to be worshiping with them. Even now, there's still some who feel, on the other side of the spectrum, that the black church is inferior to the white church. There are a lot of blacks who have been acculturated to believe that the black church is inferior. That said, I still think there's a lot of work to do. I noted this fact in my dissertation in 1995. Until I see as many white folks worshipping at black churches as I do black people worshipping at white churches, we haven't fulfilled our purpose to Christ. Generally speaking, white people still feel better than us. I even ask my white peers sometimes, remarking directly, "You think you're better than me, don't you?"

Jolted, their reply is often, "Walter, where do you get that idea?"

"You think qualitatively that just because you're white, you're better than me. I went to your schools. I worked your jobs. I've been the same places you've been. In most cases, I have better grades than you all. But even with all of that, you still feel you're better than me. The only difference is the color of my skin."

Lyndon B. Johnson once stated, "If you can convince the lowest white man he's better than the best colored man, he won't notice you're picking his pocket." This is what former President Donald Trump used to gain office and enrich his corporate benefactors with tax cuts that helped billionaires pay a lower tax rate than the working class (Saez and Zucman 2019). This same "I'm better than you" tactic has been historically espoused in American churches. When white people see the black church, they're looking at votes, not human beings with some of the same challenges, and perhaps more, than they have. They're looking at the number of people who can vote for them. They're not looking at the subset who need the most help and who probably don't vote. They never try to go out in the community and speak with them.

I have a pastor friend in Miami, and the politicians love him because they know that when they go to his church, he's going to give them a chance to say something to the congregation, guaranteeing at least 2,000 votes or so. That's the only time you'll see them attend our churches or address the community up close. Politicians have not been the only perpetrators of trying to profit from the black congregation. Sometimes it occurs from within the congregation, starting from the very top, the pastor. A popular black preacher and good friend who is now deceased would say, "When you take the profit away from the prophet, there will be no more profit." I didn't agree with money being the mission and chose to take a different approach in ministry.

There have been so many paradigm shifts that have categorized popular ministry methods and messages in the church. The first ministry type that engulfed the country was the health ministry, wherein you could be healed. That popular message had been around for years until it was replaced with the wealth gospel. I don't think much of this "prosperity gospel," as I believe it's a very deceptive reading of the Word of God. It is a misunderstanding of what Jesus intended for the church. Yes, God wants us to do well. He wants us to prosper and be in health even as our souls prosper. But He doesn't want us to hoard money or seek money as a way of fulfillment. This has been a spiritual battle in the black church for years, where a lot of mentors led their flock astray, and the mentors profited more than the members. I believe that what the Bible says about wealth is black and white, straightforward, and shouldn't be misconstrued or misinterpreted for personal gain.

In fact, the pastors that I know who did well, meaning they were effective in ministry, were not wealthy. I don't know one *effective* pastor, based on biblical standards and Christ's example, who became wealthy as a result of being a pastor. They saw the Gospel as black and white, cleaving to verses like Matthew 12:30, which reads: "This is war, and there is no neutral ground. If you're not on my side, you're the enemy; if you're not helping, you're making things worse." Because I know that "no lie comes from the truth," (1 John 2:21) some ministry matters need to remain simple and sincere, without attempts to conjure a new Gospel message.

29

CONFRONTING CANCER

I was diagnosed with Merkel cell carcinoma, a rare, deadly skin cancer, on October 31, 2003. After going through treatment, I had a bad outcome as a result of surgery to remove the cancerous growth at Sylvester Cancer Center in 2004. The surgery left me marred and disfigured. The right side of my face had a big keloid, which is a lumpy, ridged scar that occurs after a skin injury or condition has healed.

We had a couple that recently joined my church, and they were ministers who came from Bethel Baptist Church. They found it so unsightly that they decided to temporarily move their membership. Ultimately, I chose to have a cosmetic treatment to reduce the keloid. Once I had the process and growth was reduced, the couple decided to come back.

While the cancer treatment and scars may have alarmed some churchgoers, the mere diagnosis literally rocked my family. We had a Halloween party on the new property of our church, and I had just gotten back from the doctor who had done a biopsy. When I got my pathology report back about having cancer, I told my wife, and she didn't take it well. Then we decided to tell our kids that night because we were hosting the party, and they would be coming with their families. My daughter arrived first. After I told her about the diagnosis, she fainted on the spot. Afterward, my son Mark showed up with his kids. When we shared the news with him, he jumped in his car without saying a word and drove off. His silence and departure spoke volumes.

The whole ordeal was really tough on my family and the church. Despite their own fears, everyone was so supportive and encouraging, and it fueled my hope in a positive outcome. I took a trip to MD Anderson Hospital in

Houston, Texas, to get a second opinion because there was supposed to be a world-famous oncologist there. Dr. Sandra Millon-Underwood, mother of Lawrence Underwood, the guy who was playing organ for Sweet Home at that time, was on the executive board for the American Cancer Society. She knew about this doctor named Dr. Randal Weber who specialized in head and neck cancer, and she recommended him.

I was on a trip to Chicago when I got a call from Dr. Weber. He said, "I've been asked to call you. What's going on?"

I said, "I have Merkel cell carcinoma."

"Are you black?"

"Yeah," I replied with some reservation about the question.

"You probably don't have Merkel cell carcinoma, because Merkel cell carcinoma is a skin disease for white people. You tell me you're African-American, but this type of cancer probably affects less than 1% of 1% of the world's population."

I sat in silence, unsure how to reply.

"So, I'll be glad to see you. Make the arrangements. Work it out. Get here. Let me examine you, review your medical charts, all of that, and we'll go from there."

Dolores and I flew to Houston shortly thereafter. We stayed at the hospital's hotel and met him the next day. I'll never ever forget what he told me.

"Dr. Richardson," he began, "I have bad news and bad news. You have what they say you have. You have Merkel cell carcinoma. That's it."

"Okay, so what happens now?"

"Well, that's where the other bad news comes in. If surgery is performed, we can remove the cancer. If we don't do the surgery, a year from now, we won't be having a conversation. Even if we have the surgery, there's a high percentage, a good chance, that you won't be able to speak or use your voice."

He added, "You must have the surgery to save your life. But your career as a minister will be affected. We're prepared to do everything now, so you can stay here. We'll take care of you and your family while you're here. We can do everything here."

Still reeling from the stark prognosis of the surgery, I said, "Well, Doc, I need to talk to my wife. We need to talk about this."

After a short pause, I continued, "You're asking me to make a pretty tough decision right now."

Focused both on my family at home and at the church, I called the church to tell them the outcome of my visit. I talked to the chairman, and he said, "Doc, do whatever you have to do to get well. We're here and you got to get better. We're not worried about you, because you're in the best place you could be right now getting the medical attention that you need."

With that reassurance, my wife and I prepared for me to stay in Houston. Just after we made the decision to stay and do what was needed for however long it took, Dr. Weber asked, "Where are you from?"

I said, "Perrine, Florida."

"Where's Perrine?"

"Perrine," I explained, "is an area in Miami."

"My roommate when I was taking special training in oncology is the medical director for the Sylvester Cancer Center in Miami."

"Really?" I said.

"Is that close to you?"

"Yes, that's at the University of Miami."

He suggested, "Let's do this. Why don't you get the surgery there and come back here for your radiation and other treatment? We'll go back and forth until we get this straightened out."

"You mean to tell me that the guy you studied with is in Miami?"

"Yeah," he quickly offered. "Once you get the surgery done, you can decide whether or not you want to make the commute here for treatment. Or in his estimation, if he wants to keep you in Miami to do the radiation and all of that, they could do it all there in Miami."

So we ended up leaving for Miami the next day, and I had the surgery done in Miami at a Sylvester Comprehensive Cancer Center, which is right next door to Jackson Hospital. After having the surgery to remove all the cancer, I had to go back to the hospital regularly for the doctors to check my status and recovery.

There was a lady there who came from Italy to have the same kind of surgery, and because Sylvester is a research hospital, they made us test cases. We, in fact, had our surgeries on the same day. My procedure was scheduled for that afternoon, and hers was scheduled for that morning. We would end up coming back for our follow-up appointments about the same time on every occasion. She would go in first, and I would go in second at each appointment. For the first couple of times we went there, we would talk about how we were faring with the surgical side effects. I was swelling up very badly, and she had some residual effects as well. However, none of it affected the way she looked. She was still a very beautiful lady and hailed from a prominent background in Italy, I later discovered.

I went back for my routine follow-up appointment one day, looking forward to chatting with her, but she was not there. I asked my doctor about her whereabouts, and he replied, "Let's talk about that once we're all done. Let me check you out."

When he was done checking on me and recording his voice notes in a small recording device, he said, "She's not doing well."

"What do you mean she's not doing well?"

"She's ill. And you are a minister, so you need to pray for her."

"She's not doing well as a result of the Merkel cell carcinoma?" I quizzed him, wanting to get complete clarity.

"Yes."

I became solemn, concerned about both of us.

The next time I went back for an appointment, I didn't see her again. However, this time, I waited to ask about her whereabouts at the end of my appointment. I asked my doctor how she was doing, and he announced solemnly, "She didn't make it."

A week later, following that announcement, I was reading the *Miami Herald* and saw that a famous musician named Joe Zawinul had died. I met Joe in 1965 when I first visited Tallahassee with the man who drove me to school the following year. We went to the Savoy Nightclub and Cannonball Adderly was playing there with his brother Nat, and he had a white keyboard player named Joe Zawinul. I got to meet him and the entire jazz ensemble that night.

The newspaper's headline read: "Famous Jazz Pianist Joe Zawinul Dead." I read the entire article because of my former interaction with him. To my dismay, he died from Merkel cell carcinoma, which is the cancer I had. At that moment, I remembered what Dr. Weber told me about this being one of the most aggressive forms of skin cancer there is. My friend from Italy didn't make it. Joe didn't make it. Nevertheless, for some strange reason, and I said this to my congregation, God left me here. There's a purpose for me still being here.

One of the church trustees, Jesse Tyson, came to talk to me about my plan for the future just in case something happened where I would not be able to complete the time that God had given me as a pastor. He asked whether I had I given any thought to retirement. I had thought about it and felt secure because I had pretty good coffers from working at Sears. The church had taken out a significant amount of my salary towards retirement, but he thought we should be a little bit more aggressive. Sweet Home membership and attendance was growing exponentially at the time. In his mind, I probably wasn't making the kind of money I should make. Based on other ministerial leaders and executives, I needed to be treated as well as they were being treated. So he not only pushed the trustee board for a retirement package, but a better salary for me. That was my first time in being pastor that I tackled retirement planning. He said, "Find out from your financial planner what it would take for you to maintain your current salary if you retired, at least 80% of that."

Confronted with premature retirement, I was able to report to him what my financial planner had advised, which was a fairly high amount.

"Well, we'll work towards that," he said.

Six years after that conversation and after 27 years in church ministry, I decided to step down as pastor in 2010, choosing to focus instead on family, music projects, and as always, community involvement. One of the young kids at church came up to me with his mother one Sunday before my official departure and said, "I love to hear you preach. I love to hear you preach." He was giddy, and his words flowed easily from a pure sincerity.

"Thank you, son," I said. "Thank you so much. You don't know what that does to me."

"I hate to see you go," he added.

"Well, you know, there comes a time when all of us have to retire from these jobs that we have, and pastoring is a job, believe it or not."

"Can I ask you something?"

"Sure, you can ask me anything."

"Why do you scream when you preach?" His mother looked at him like, *don't ask him that.*

In an attempt to help her save face and respond to him with reciprocal sincerity, I replied, "That's a good question, young man. The reason I scream now, and I've been screening for a few years now, is because a few years ago, I was not supposed to be able to talk anymore. I had cancer. Even though I don't scream like I used to, I still have the ability to scream. So every time you hear me screaming, it's really me thanking God for the privilege to be able to scream because cancer didn't kill me."

30

THE TRANSITION

U nlike many other Baptist churches, the chairman of the board really ran the church. Deacon Rudolph Simmons had told me, "Everything that you ever wanted to do in ministry, you can do it right here at Sweet Home Baptist Church." I was fortunate to have this Deacon Simmons in my corner throughout my time as pastor. He died on February 6, 2006, and this greatly impacted me and the ministry, influencing when and why I retired. He would miss the Miami-Dade County proclamation of "Dr. Walter T. Richardson Day" in September 2006. He had been with me throughout my evolution as head pastor, relishing my civic honors and church development. I would surely miss him both personally and professionally.

At age 24, Rudolph Simmons, Sr. moved to West Perrine from Tennille, Georgia, in 1949, following a two-year stint in the United States Army. Dade County offered much better employment opportunities than the small rural city of Tennille. He and his wife, Ollie, and their small son, Rudolph Jr., started visiting Sweet Home as soon as it was organized. The charter members and early "joiners" loved this young family and embraced them because young Simmons was a dutiful usher, and Ollie could sing beautifully. In 1954, Simmons and Herbert Gillis were ordained as the first new deacons of the church. Simmons rose quickly in that circle of church leaders, although the membership was quite small.

There were three other Baptist churches in West Perrine: Mount Moriah Missionary Baptist, Mount Sinai Missionary Baptist, St. Peter's Baptist Missionary Baptist Church. Mount Moriah Missionary Baptist Church was the oldest and the largest. All of Sweet Home's deacons had left that church over a disagreement regarding the pastor, Rev. William Edcar. Mt. Sinai was the second largest church. Another Baptist church, St. Peter's, would simultaneously emerge along the same time as Sweet Home, and it had a primarily Bahamian base. That church took its name from disciple Peter's quarters where many seasonal laborers lived.

When I arrived as pastor in October 1983, Deacon Simmons was the chairman of the board. He literally ran everything in the church. This short, quick-walking, dark-skinned, jovial man led devotion and prayer, moderated all church meetings, purchased ministry supplies, and took the church receipts to the bank, occasionally keeping the money in the trunk of his car until Monday when he and Deacon Edward Jordan could make deposits at Dixie National Bank. He basically did everything except preach at Sweet Home.

The pulpit had been vacant since April 1983, and the church wanted a new spiritual leader. The original pastor, Elzie King, resigned for personal reasons after having served for a little over 20 years. Reverend James Allen subsequently resigned after seven years as the church's pastor. When Deacon Simmons learned about me from Sis. Kay Bertha Collins, a member of Second Baptist Church where I was serving as an associate pastor, and from his daughter-in-law Ruthie Simmons, who worked with me as Sears, he sought me out. He would come by Sears almost daily to talk with me. He did not want another pastor for Sweet Home that had less education than he.

When I read my vision for Sweet Home at my first monthly business meeting as pastor in November 1983 and announced the church's motto, *"The church that is moving up and reaching out,"* I received lengthy and enthusiastic applause. Deacon Simmons came to the microphone and said, "Congregation, we have heard from our pastor. Let us govern ourselves accordingly." Now, what that meant to the congregation was that Deacon Simmons fully supported the new pastor. What it meant to me was that unless Deacon Simmons supported that vision, I was going to have some challenges with the church leadership. Deacon Simmons ran everything in the church. What he said, went, what he did mattered, and who he supported, succeeded.

The church had deacons and they had trustees, but one had to be a trustee in order to be a deacon. So, all the deacons were trustees, and then there were others who were just trustees. They had absolutely no power;

they were just there to help do the physical work at the church, such as trimming the trees and painting. All decisions had to be approved by the deacons, not the trustees.

However, I made sure that they were two distinct bodies that had two distinct ministries. Together, they would comprise the Board of Directors or the Governing Board of the church, but they weren't completely independent of each other. I explained the new direction of a modern ministry, wherein the deacons' role was strictly spiritual. They would take care of and oversee the welfare of church members, as well as their social needs. The deacons were to be part of everything that all the ministries did in terms of setting their budgets so they could operate in excellence. They were to ensure that people who needed pastoral care were attended to, providing communion at church and visits to the sick. That was the role of the deacons. The trustees were solely responsible for the fiscal and physical operations of the church. That was it. Once I got that separation, we held true it. So that while they both worked together because they had to know what the other was doing, they served different functions. I even narrowed it to the point that there were only three trustees and three deacons who would be part of the church Executive Committee. In this way, no one board had all the votes.

I suggested and it was accepted that my sister-in-law, Brenda Williams, become a member of the trustee board. She brought a great balance, because while she was in favor of a lot of things that happened, she always sensitized them to my input, saying, "We wouldn't be where we are financially or otherwise without the leadership of our pastor. Let's make sure that he's considered and his opinions are considered, and everything that we're doing is based on his philosophy of ministry and that we're really not working independent of his voice and his vision." That was the balance she brought to that board.

The church's constitution and bylaws were dated, and the ministry was not incorporated. The church was spelled "Sweethome" as one word at the time. Meanwhile, I had it noted a different way spelled as two words: Sweet Home. The original name, owned by the deacons, trustees and successors, was the way the church was known. The one-word phrase, however, raised many questions for me. In addition, I had received mail directly to the church addressing the deacons and trustees, and I didn't know what that meant as a legal entity. I explained my point of reference about updating the ministry until at least the entity was fully incorporated and the bylaws reflected current best practices. Deacon Simmons took me to meet a Jewish lawyer who had helped the church when the previous pastor changed the church bylaws, and had been terminated as a result. Attorney Sanford Dernis was a strategic, wise, discerning man who understood what the church needed and how he needed to draft documents to accommodate this. By 1989, Sweet Home Baptist Church was incorporated with a modified spelling (two words) and ready to conduct business in a more customary fashion. Without Deacon Simmons, none of these enhancements would have happened. Even though he was not formally trained or educated in religion or business administration, he had good common sense and was open to new ideas to make the church more compatible to what was happening in society.

The church membership grew exponentially, from fewer than 100 active members when I arrived to well over 1,500 when I retired. On Sundays, there was literally no room for parking, as the church's property was less than an acre. Members and visitors had to park in other people's driveways, in the nearby park's limited spaces, or on private property.

At that point, a timely decision was made to consider a larger plot of land for Sweet Home, and there were 13 acres of land available just two blocks from Sweet Home's one-acre plot. We needed a new facility, and we needed a loan. Although the church had been collecting building fund gifts, a new project involving the hiring of an architect and eventually a construction company required much more money than we had in our coffers. Deacon Simmons and I visited Dixie National Bank as a result.

By the time we made the decision to purchase 24 acres of land for more ministry expansion in 2005, Deacon Simmons was no longer part of the decision-making. Since my arrival at the church, he had been part of every major decision at Sweet Home. When I returned from MD Anderson from cancer treatment in February 2006, Deacon Simmons died. He transitioned from this world two years following my cancer surgery and three years before we marched into the new church. He gave his final approval on every prospective deacon and church administrative decision. We always discussed everything in my office, and I can still remember some of his catchphrases, such as: "the same jack that jacks up, jacks down," "starched and ironed," and "pray with him, church."

His saying about "the same jack that jacks up, jacks down" meant that everything is two-sided. No situation has just one side, so you need to look at issues from both or all sides. That was his kind of catchall expression for handling conflicts because he recognized that in a conflict, there are always at least two opinions or perspectives. When Deacon Simmons said "starched and ironed," he meant you needed to be clean and ready to be presented. Historically, when a black man went to church on Sunday, he would be wearing overalls with a dress shirt, and the shirt would be washed and starched with Argo starch — so much so that the shirt was stiff after ironing. Thus, this phrase meant that you're ready to be presented in church in a formal way.

When I'd be preaching and get towards the end of my sermon, Deacon Simmons would shout, "Pray with him, church!" That meant it was time for me to kind of go into praise and celebration mode. He would feel it coming, and he would say, "Pray with him, church." This signaled the congregation that the amens needed to be a little bit more emphasized, and we needed to make a little bit more noise to show support to the pastor's message.

As the church began to expand in size and influence, Deacon Simmons and others like him who had been around from the beginning began to become less influential because they lacked formal training or experience in the church's business needs, especially related to real estate. We were dealing with situations like land purchases and other significant governance and financial matters at the time. Attorney Dernis was our go-to person for legal matters, and others like both Al Dotson, Jr. and Sr., the first African-American store manager for Sears Roebuck & Company, along with Jesse Tyson, the Marketing Director and President of Exxon Mobil Inter-American, provided great insight and influence. Tony Rogers was also a board member who was able to parlay his corporate experience to help the church maneuver through developmental needs triggered from growth.

We planned on buying a large plot of land on the corner of Southwest 184th and 107th Avenue to build a new church. The Dotsons and Jesse Tyson were pivotal in working through the land deal. They understood contracts and had great communication skills. Thus, they were able to aptly deal with the people who owned the property. Joshua K. Dove, who was a retired educator from the Richmond Heights area, along with other trustees like Richard Wiggins, also helped with negotiating the purchase of the land. Although he wasn't at the forefront, Deacon Simmons was also part of this transaction. Ultimately, we were able to purchase 24 acres for $1.2 million. Before we moved into Sweet Home, we had an offer to purchase 10 of those acres of the land for $6 million.

There were some who felt that Sweet Home, going into its next phase, needed a younger pastor who could grow with the new church, the "New Sweet Home," as some suggested. The number of people who felt that way was small, but they were influential. They talked to me informally about the plans I had for retirement. By the time the church had formally moved into its new location, the advent of my retirement was a serious consideration.

When I was first confronted with the prospect of retirement in 2003, I was 56. I had come back from my battle with Merkel cell cancer, there were thoughts about, "Is this guy going to be okay for the future? Should we be planning for, even if it takes years, his retirement?" I started seriously looking at my income options. I was teaching at the university and had earned my doctorate, so I could have easily supplemented my retirement income from the church. Someone said, "You know, even people like Dr. Mack King Carter have been talking to the same financial advisor that you have about the future. And I think he wants to do what his predecessor did and retire at age 60." This was a profound statement because the late Dr. Carter was the influential pastor of the megachurch New Mount Olive Baptist Church in Fort Lauderdale. Apparently, he encountered a challenge from the church trustees and some deacons after they became dissatisfied with his leadership and tried to force his retirement.

In 2009, the same year we marched into our new church, the conversation about my retirement became more vocal, with people saying, "Pastor, you've been sick, there's no guarantee that you're not going to get sick again." Some in the congregation felt that they needed to attract younger members with a young pastor, and they would explicitly ask, "Do you have any plans for retirement?"

I answered, "Not immediately. Why are you raising this question now?"

During that time, there was a lot of angst because word got out beyond the board that I was considering retirement. Most people who attended Sweet Home did not want me to leave. I would say 95 percent of the people there didn't want me to even consider leaving at that time. Some trustees from Sweet Home, such as Inez Mitchell, asked me to consider starting my own ministry.

We were in a new church with greater opportunities to expand. Still, I gave them permission and my blessing to at least start looking at our options to see who could become the new pastor. Meanwhile, Tyson, Dotson Sr., and I began working up my retirement package. We came to the understanding that whenever I left Sweet Home, I would be paid in the form of an annuity that would fund me for the rest of my life, assuming I would live to age 85 and perhaps even beyond.

So, I had hired a guy named Emory Berry right out of seminary. He was a member of the AME tradition at that time. I had swayed him away from the AME church to be a Baptist pastor with me. He was also a product of Second Baptist Church, my former church. So he knew me, and I knew his family well. We had met at Harvard in 2004 after a good friend and fraternity brother named Pastor G. Vincent Lewis told me about a summer internship at Harvard Divinity Leadership School. He said it was an opportunity for scholarly people who had at least a master's, but preferably a doctorate degree. He thought I would benefit from attending. It was a competitive program, and they only selected 50 people from around the world to participate each year. My friend explained that this was probably going to be their last class and asked whether I was interested. Once I told him that I was very much interested, he said he could probably get me a scholarship, which he did. And so it turned out that I got a scholarship. My expenses that I had to pay outside of my scholarship were taken care of by Sweet Home. I met 49 wonderful people from around the world who came to Harvard to study for the summer. Some very significant people were there that summer, including pastors from some very erudite churches. I got a chance to rub elbows with some of the best thinkers in social justice, religious reform, and ethical issues.

The discussions were educational and inspirational, often challenging commonly-held beliefs about every aspect of ministry and its practical impact on society. They also discussed ways to drive the church forward economically. The internship lasted for only two weeks, but it almost felt like a lifetime because we would work from early in the morning, starting at 6 a.m., until past midnight for the entire time. We were really cramming. Most had done this kind of work before, since most of us had our doctorates, which requires intense research and study. No matter the familiarity with the work ethic, it was a life-changing experience, at least for me.

I contacted Emory to see what his plans were in ministry. He was very bright, and I felt he had a lot of promise. In a conversation with Tony Rogers, he asked, "Well, who would you consider being a replacement for you if you were to retire?" I initially thought of Emory, but I felt he wasn't ready to lead a congregation of that size. He would be better suited as head pastor of a smaller congregation where he could learn and develop administrative skills. Sweet Home was not a first pastor church, so to speak. We needed someone with experience pastoring a church, especially of that size.

When I told him that I had no one in mind, he asked, "What about current people? What about former members of your staff?"

So, we talked about our youth pastor, Joseph Turner, as a possibility. We talked about another young pastor, who was my mentee, named Norman Freeman. We also talked about a few other people, but at that point, I was not convinced that any of them could continue the ministry work that I had started. All of them were loyal to their current ministries, and I didn't think they would be remotely interested in leaving what they were doing to come to Sweet Home. There was a different kind of vibe at the church, and Sweet Home was becoming more top heavy with people of means. Even though we were still in Perrine, the traditional services were changing. We had fewer deacons singing hymns and adopted the contemporary nuances of black worship services. For instance, we had a praise team instead of the choir ushering in a new form of worship, which was working well.

To complement the current direction of the church, I suggested we launch a national search for a new pastor. "I think there may be some talent out there that we're overlooking," I said. The board agreed to this, and then we began a nation-wide search. The three young local pastors we initially approached — Norman Freeman, Joe Turner, and Emory Berry — all expressed interest. Freeman and Turner had worked as youth pastors, and Berry was the current minister of education. However, in my opinion, they weren't excited about the idea of coming back to Sweet Home in the capacity of head pastor within the current church structure.

In May 2009, we had a church meeting, and I was asked pointedly, "Are we going to go forward with looking for a new pastor or do you want to stay?" In front of a packed church, I made the decision, announcing, "I'm ready for retirement." As a result, there was a pastoral search committee organized, and they were given the responsibility to identify a new pastor.

When we went national, we had a lot of people interested in becoming the new pastor. Sweet Home had national acclaim because of all the community work we've done and the major affiliations we had developed to impact the community at large. People around the country also knew me for my music as a two-time Grammy nominated musician. Our church's name was out there, needless to say. The committee went through a number of candidates, but by the end of the year, no one had been deemed satisfactory for the position. Timing was crucial, though, because we had agreed that the church would start paying me in January 2010 for retirement through the annuity they had bought for me. The church board asked whether I would stay on as pastor beyond December 31, 2009, until they found someone new. The other option was to get an interim pastor and allow me to begin my retirement as planned. Overwhelmingly, they asked me to stay on until further notice. We had momentum with the church growing rapidly, and to potentially stop or interrupt it to bring on an interim pastor and then a new pastor, could have been catastrophic to the ministry. Thus, I stayed on as pastor during that time.

The committee soon narrowed down the search to two gentlemen: one from California and one from Georgia. Jeremy Upton from Atlanta, Georgia, got more committee votes than the other gentleman. At the time, he was working for the late Bishop Eddie Long of New Birth as his executive pastor in charge of new church plants. Young and very smart, he was a good preacher who had graduated number one in his class from Morehouse College as an undergraduate. I preached my last sermon at Sweet Home on April 4, 2010, Easter Sunday, and he took over as head pastor on April 5, 2010.

31

NEW HOME

After I preached my last sermon as pastor at Sweet Home, I took a very long, deep breath. I was physically drained and emotionally exhausted from pastoring. After commandeering three successful building projects, involving the ministry in viable community endeavors, and assisting the ministry through a tenuous selection process for my successor, I needed a break. Dolores and I decided to take the next Sunday off and not attend services anywhere, although we had been invited to worship at other places. I was advised not to attend Sweet Home, as a visit from the former pastor could be distracting.

After all, Dolores and I knew that we'd be embraced and welcomed enthusiastically, not coddled necessarily, but at least acknowledged as the "pastor emeritus." It was understood I would not be a part of the administrative responsibilities of the church going forward, neither would I have any input as it relates to what was going to be taught nor the direction of the church, but we also knew that was our family and had been our family for 27 years.

The church arranged an elaborate, formal retirement dinner for me on May 1, 2010, at Doral Country Club, which is now the Trump Country Club. The late U.S. Attorney General Janet Reno was the main speaker at my retirement dinner. She was a good friend who became an "honorary" member of the church before she became the attorney general under President Bill Clinton. Throughout the years, she had been a frequent visitor and contributor to the ministry. The event, which was held in the large community room, was packed with church members, high school and college classmates, and fraternity brothers, as well as notable people I had worked with in the community and political sphere. My second book, "Think on These things," had come out on April 4th, the day of my last sermon, and we had copies available for sale for guests at the dinner.

Along with a few relatively new but significant faces, Jeremy Upton attended my retirement dinner with his wife, Brianna. It became obvious to me after having initial conversations with the new pastor that I was probably going to be minimized once he took the helm. Even at my retirement gathering, where he was given a chance to offer remarks and a prayer, he was very frank about his intentions to eliminate my involvement in the church. So I asked, "When do you want us to return to Sweet Home after giving you a chance to get settled in your role as a pastor? I don't want people to look at me in church and say, 'How does that resonate with Pastor Richardson?'" I continued, "You know, you and I should agree that perhaps I shouldn't come back immediately."

He said, "I totally agree with that because these new sheep need to hear my voice."

I said, "No problem. When do you want me to come back to Sweet Home?"

"Give me a month or two," he responded.

"So, you mean by the end of July?" I deduced, because it was May.

"Yeah," he said, "give me that long."

"No problem," I said, "Well, listen, I'm here for you. If you need to run anything by me in terms of historical information, feel free to do that."

"Okay, no problem at all."

Shortly thereafter, notice was issued for his formal installation as pastor, but I was not invited to participate. And since there were no models and best practices for retired pastors attending services at their former church, I may have been anxious, ignorantly so, about my non-involvement. I did eventually get an informal invite to be there just as part of the audience. I had no role to present, reflect, or speak in any form. And from his perspective, it would have been best if I didn't even show up, so the congregation could focus solely on him. I imagine it was the notion that out of sight would mean out of mind. Nevertheless, I showed up, because I thought that was the courteous thing to do in formally passing the baton in some capacity.

On the day of the installation, there were three rows of seats in the pulpit. Jeremy, along with the speaker and the MC, sat on the first row. Behind them was a row of people who were formally invited. Once I arrived, they made room for me on the third row in the pulpit. Still, I was not asked to do or say anything during the installation service.

Jeremy made several major changes after the installation, including altering the name of the church. On the Sunday after he was formally made pastor, he changed the name on the tithing envelopes to "Sweet Home Church" instead of Sweet Home Missionary Baptist Church. The word "missionary" and "Baptist" were intentionally removed. In respect to the new pastor, I was not in attendance, but I got a phone call from one of the deacons. He asked, "What do we do? This is not the direction we thought the church was going to go."

I advised, "Well, you all need to talk to the pastor and come to an understanding of what everybody's role is. If that has not happened, it needs to happen now."

They did have a meeting with the pastor, and afterward, the church name was changed back on the envelopes. Although resolved, there was still some tension because the new pastor came in with a unilateral mindset, believing he could make the final decisions without sanction or even input. He came out of the late Bishop Eddie Long's church in metropolitan Atlanta, where that sort of autonomous decision-making was the norm.

I think Pastor Upton felt his authority was being challenged when a couple of older members of Sweet Home died, and they had indicated to their families that the person that was going to funeralize or eulogize them should be the former pastor, talking about me. To that, Pastor Upton reminded the congregation that I was the former pastor, and even though I would be eulogizing these members, I still had no authority in the church. Even for the church's anniversary, which came up six months after I retired, I was not involved at all. Most of the speakers came from out of town. I was aware that in many other settings where a pastor was still actively preaching and/or was the pastor emeritus, that this would be one of the times when he would necessarily be involved.

Almost immediately upon Pastor Upton's arrival at Sweet Home, the church administration was completely overturned. A new executive pastor, Theo Johnson, was hired. A young lady who came out of the corporate business arena from a major organization was brought in as the chief operating officer of the church. I don't believe she was a minister at that time, but she may have been given a license to become a minister at the church. She was apparently very sharp with a great corporate mindset. However, some of her new policies, procedures, and practices were not "black church" oriented. The service itself had already changed. We had less of the hymn singing by the deacons, and we moved to the new nuances of black worship, including having a praise team rather than a choir to lead worship during Sunday services.

After Deacon Simmons died, the church didn't have the benefit of that old time religion and reverent attitude about former pastors and church transitions. The church no longer possessed that mother wit, shoot-from-the-hip wisdom he provided. Instead, the church was heavily influenced by the professional organizational exposure of the new, highly educated members who were all well-recognized in their circles and spheres of influence. So, the people who had blue-collar backgrounds like Deacon Simmons were waning in terms of their presence and influence.

Like Deacon Simmons, who had enculturated and lovingly embraced me, Sweet Home embraced the Reverend Jeremy Upon because it was widely believed that of the two finalists for pastor, I endorsed him. When he won the election as pastor, I told the church to support, love, and appreciate him. Without that encouragement and left to their own devices, I believe the church members would have resisted or reversed course sooner than they ultimately did. In fact, he probably would not have lasted the year and a half that he was there otherwise.

When Pastor Upton left the church after being asked to resign, he took a substantial number of members with him because a lot of people didn't know the backstory and thought Sweet Home, in some regard, had done him wrong. There was a lot of behind-the-scenes drama that was never made public, so the church members didn't know. Even in the situations that did come to light, such as changing the church's name on the envelopes, many church members may not have understood the real motivation behind them. Those who left with him started meeting at various other places until they got their own place in Homestead, Florida. And through those multiple changes in venue, many who left with Jeremy Upton came back to Sweet Home. Theo Johnson, the executive pastor who came on to assist Pastor Upton, is now the senior pastor at Sweet Home Missionary Baptist Church.

32

WELL DONE

My tenure as pastor of Sweet Home afforded me the opportunity to impact not just the congregation, but also local and even national communities of faith who sought to do the same thing we did: change lives and impact the community through ministry. In doing so, I have met and interacted with many dignitaries, including presidents, carrying out their broader aims that would leave generational impact through missionary work around the world. Like me, these men and women may have been imperfect, but they were perfectly suited for their calling to advance the faith through their influence.

President George W. Bush's first executive order established the Office of Faith-Based and Community Initiatives in the White House, allowing smaller and more overtly religious groups to receive government funding for providing social services (President and His Faith — The Faith-Based Initiative Controversy, 2004). President Bush awarded funds, in this regard, to communities of faith in his home state of Texas and in other states like Florida. The government trusted that if they gave these funds to particularly large or influential local religious ministries, the church would disperse these funds throughout the communities. They identified a pastor from West Palm Beach to provide financial support as needed for communities in Florida. Among those who were awarded these funds was Pastor T.D. Jakes and Pastor Kirbyjon Caldwell. The guy from Florida allegedly kept all the money for himself instead of sharing it with the community. As a result, for the next round of funds disbursement, he was excluded. In finding his replacement in Florida, I was contacted and extended an invitation to go to D.C. for a meeting with the President in 2006. When I got there, I met

Bishop Eddie Long from Georgia and others, but I was the only person from Florida. I was expected to be the community liaison, or connection, to ensure that the funds could be accessed for those faith-based organizations or initiatives that would support the communities' needs. Sweet Home was allocated some of the funds to continue its community work, and the majority went to programs that supported literacy, economic growth, and the kinds of initiatives that we talked about when I went to Harvard.

Similarly, the Ford Foundation was interested in missionary work because of its Senior Program Officer and Program Officer, Linetta Gilbert, who was very religious. She funded the grant for our missionary efforts, called Faith Partnerships, in West Africa. Diana Jones Wilson was the president and founder of the organization, and she was elemental in uniting the various black Christian churches for this effort. Most of the people who had become missionaries in Africa, particularly in countries like Ghana, were white missionaries who brought their own brand of Christianity. With the foundation's support, we aimed to provide a corrective course to some of the unsuitable things that had happened throughout the years. So, I was one of several pastors, many of whom were scholars, who went to take a look at what was happening on the continent and to offer some feedback as to what we could do to rectify, or at least address, some of the errors to global Christianity through the American lens.

I also got a chance to visit Soweto, which is an acronym for South-Western Townships, while in Africa. I got a chance to see Nelson Mandela's house, but he wasn't there at the time. He resided in the South African President's mansion, and so his house was still there but occupied by family. I also visited South Africa proper and Johannesburg.

During our two weeks there in 2007, our team was able to thoroughly accomplish our assessment and plans for intervention. We came away knowing that we had made an impact by providing some sustenance to the programs that provide resources to that region of the world. Most of our impact was helping the guide churches with outreach efforts in Africa in order to give them an idea of what could happen if, in fact, we put our heads and hearts together.

Later in 2007, I would come into contact with another soon-to-be legendary leader, Barack Obama. I got an unexpected phone call asking me whether I would provide the invocation for (at that time) Senator Obama because he was going to be coming to Miami. The excitement about the potential election of America's first black president was captivating media attention worldwide. Obama was the Harvard-educated son of a black father from Kenya and a white mother from Kansas. He was going to be at the Intercontinental Hotel for an event hosted by the Latin Builders Association. Somebody asked me if I spoke any Spanish, and I explained that I could speak Spanish fluently. So, when I got to the hotel and it was time for the prayer, I delivered the invocation in both Spanish and English. Impressed by the duality, someone from the Obama campaign called to ask me about doing the invocation just before he was to head into the final stretch before the presidential election. This was to take place in Bayfront Park, which is across from the Intercontinental Hotel. Win or lose for Obama, I saw this as a historical moment, so I gladly accepted.

I subsequently met him again because I did some work with the Secret Service. As a result, I was able to meet him in 2013 while in his second term as president. This year was especially challenging for me because I had surgery for prostate cancer. Despite that, I was honored to be able to encounter this brilliant leader again in my lifetime. I was among four people who had a private meeting with President Obama during one of his visits to Miami. One of the other people was a motorcycle officer who had been leading Obama's motorcade and was struck by a car and injured. He wasn't completely recovered, but he healed up well enough to come to that meeting on Miami Beach. He was there being honored by the President. There were also two lawyers present who had handled a case involving the Secret Service. I was there because I had provided ministerial counseling to some agents who had done some things wrong and given some advice to Paula Reid who was, at that time, the Secret Service Director for the South American region (Leonnig & Nakamura, 2012). My gift for doing that was this meeting and a photo-op with President Obama.

During this time, I had again been diagnosed with cancer on March 29, 2013. This time, it was prostate cancer. I was alarmed but not in despair—I had already seen God's miraculous hand in my life, and I knew He'd be in control again with this health bout. I had surgery on July 12, 2013. I had considered alternative options before surgery. First, because my PSA was 0.4 and my Gleason score was 6 based on my biopsy, I had the option of active surveillance rather than surgery. Dr. Mumford indicated that there was a good chance that I could die *with* the disease, but not *from* the disease if I decided to do nothing. The other options were radiation with either radioactive seeds or direct radiation to the prostrate over a six-week period. The final other option was the elimination of the prostate by open surgery or robotic surgery. Of the options considered, the least intrusive with the best outcome was the robotic removal of the prostate. I was referred to Dr. Sanjay Razdan, a popular urologist, who was a master surgeon with the Da Vinci Robot.

After a series of preparation protocols with my family present, I underwent the surgery. I went in on Friday morning, was operated on Friday afternoon, recovered overnight, and was released Saturday around noon. For the next six weeks, I was advised not to lift anything heavier than 10 pounds. My catheter was removed after nine days. My incontinence stopped after 3 weeks. I resumed my regular activities after six weeks, including walking, running, and playing golf. I resumed my speaking engagements, and community activities as well.

In many circles, I would be called driven, but I enjoy motivating and encouraging others to keep going. My grandson went back to college after taking a break, and I urged him to get back in school. I told him, "I'm going to call you every day until you walk across that stage," and I've done that. Now he gets that I'm the kind of person who can drive someone to success, and I'm driving him. Like me, he pledged Omega Psi Phi fraternity.

While at FAMU, I started the Omega undergraduate pledge process but had to abandon it once I left school. I joined the Masons when I was in the military, but I kind of let that go, too, once I became a civilian. One day in 1995, I think, I approached an Omega Psi Phi Fraternity leader who was a member of my church and who later became the Grand Basileus (or chief executive) about becoming "a Que." Never truly comfortable with leaving an important assignment incomplete, I went ahead and completed an application to start my initiation process for the grad chapter of Omega Psi Phi. As a Que at any level, our goal remains the same: uplift the lives of mankind through community service and civic involvement.

On January 20, 1996, I met with several members of the Pi Nu Chapter at the Richmond Elementary School in Miami for what I thought was another session to prepare me for initiation. After a few preliminary actions that evening, I was formally initiated into the Omega family, becoming the first member of my family to do so, as all the men in the Richardson family had pledged Alpha Phi Alpha. Some present on that unforgettable night were Joshua K. Dove, James "Buddha" Gooden, and George Grace. In July 1996, my wife and I traveled to Los Angeles, California, for my first conclave as an Omega man. While at the conclave, I became a part of the Que Chorale. Although I sang with the chorale that year, I offered my assistance to the aging and less agile accompanist during one of our rehearsals. He and I took turns playing for the chorale during performances.

I was given a committee assignment when I first became a member in '96. After serving on several fraternity committees, I was chosen to be the basileus for my local chapter in 1999. Within two years, I ended up being the state chaplain of Florida, and then a few years later, I became the district chaplain who is in charge of all chaplains and chaplaincy services for four states: Georgia, Florida, Mississippi, and Alabama. That role put me on the map with the fraternity, because now everyone in the country got a chance to know more about what was happening with the seventh and largest district due to my entrenched civic affiliations. It happens to be the largest district primarily because most of the Southern schools are located in these four states.

During a trip to Shanghai, China, with my fraternity in 2018, the new Grand Basileus, Dr. David Marion, selected me as Grand Chaplain of Omega Psi Phi Fraternity, Inc. I had served as chaplain several times throughout my career, including for the Miami Dade Police Department in 1989, when I became the first black person to serve in that role. Serving as chaplain for the Miami Dolphins football team was my shortest tenure. Like many athletes, they are a superstitious bunch, so after they lost their first two games with me as chaplain and praying over them, they announced that they no longer needed my services. Meanwhile, my tenure as national chaplain with my fraternity is a four-year commitment, lasting until 2022.

I spend a lot of my time working as the spiritual director of the fraternity. Monday through Sunday, I'm on the phone every day offering prayers. Every week, there's some need with the fraternity to which I must respond. Of the 23,000 members worldwide, we have about half, or about 11,000, who are active in their prayer life, wanting to maintain their spiritual equilibrium so to speak. We have 750 chapters across the world, and I've been to many of them as part of my work.

Like my father and his father before him, I have dedicated most of my life to ministry through the church, community organizations, my fraternity, and even my employment. When my father, Walter H. Richardson, died on January 14, 2023, at age 100, my inspiration for service changed, for he represented a standard of duty that I always admired. During his funeral service, my son Mark gave a special tribute to his grandfather, recalling a story of when my father missed his high school graduation. Mark explained how he was extremely hurt because my father, his "buddy," had never missed an important event in his life. He said, "Everything I accomplished in life, my grandaddy was there."

As our family cheered loudly when his name was called and he received his diploma in hand, Mark scanned the audience where we were seated to see if his grandfather was able to make it. When he saw no sign of his granddaddy, his joy of accomplishment quickly dissipated to lingering disappointment. After the graduation ceremony, I handed Mark an envelope addressed to him. He retrieved a check in the envelope made out to him with "lots of zeros," and on the memo line, it read: "Job Well Done."

Mark recalled how "tired" he was after attending school for 13 years of studies combined with both routine academic and church activities. His grandfather writing those three words to him "meant everything" on the occasion of his graduation because my father had witnessed the many responsibilities that Mark had. Similarly, Mark culminated his funeral tribute with saying "well done" to his grandfather, who had spent most of his adult life supporting a family, church, and community. My father had founded two other church locations in Belle Glade, Fla., and Valdosta, Ga. Both were named The Church of God Tabernacle. As a leader, he was compassionate toward the less fortunate and joined efforts to support victims of natural disasters in the U.S. and abroad, including Africa and the Caribbean. Upon his death, Mark noted during his speech, "My granddaddy graduated. He was tired... so he graduated." He added that when his granddaddy got to heaven, his Father handed him a package, and in the memo section of a blank check, it said, "Job Well Done."

As I reflect on my life's journey, my hope is that my father felt the same about my ministry work. Thus, my inspiration is no longer driven by a sense of responsibility to others; it is motivated by a desire to hear those same words spoken about me in passing: "Well done."

33

AIN'T GOT TIRED YET

My first published sermon was titled "The Half Has Not Been Told." It initially came out on cassette tape, and then later on CD. It was a popular Black History Month sermon that I delivered around 1989. The premise is based on the Queen of Sheba's meeting with King Solomon. She did not believe what she had been told about this man's wisdom and wealth. After she got a chance to meet him and see his kingdom, she said, "However I did not believe the words until I came and saw with my own eyes; and indeed the half was not told me. Your wisdom and prosperity exceed the fame of which I heard" (1 Kings 10:7 NKJV). Because it was so popular, we published it on CD in 1993.

I'm a fifth-generation preacher who has served in ministry for 52 years, and as a result, I have met and prayed with civic leaders and dignitaries worldwide. I even met Kamala Harris in 2019 when she was running for Vice President of the United States alongside President Joe Biden. I have ministered in various forms, especially through music over the years. Now, in pseudo-retirement, I spend my time continuing to advise, minister, and serve my community. My fraternity responsibilities keep me busy with prayer requests and spiritual advising. Meanwhile, I continue to record music while serving on various boards. In terms of my life, the half has not been told.

When I became the pastor of Sweet Home, I made sure that I got involved with what was called the Miami-Dade Community Relations Board (CRB). Rev. Ferguson had been on the board and was aware of its impact, and he thought that it would be an ideal opportunity for me to get involved in helping black folks countywide. The board was established in

1963 because, up until that time, there were separate beaches and public facilities for blacks in and around Dade County. Blacks, in many cases, because of county ordinances, did not enjoy the same civic and social privileges. The first year, the culturally diverse board included prominent members like Archbishop Coleman Carroll, Rabbi Solomon Schiff, Henry King Stanford, president of the University of Miami, and Rev. Edward Graham, pastor of Mount Zion Baptist Church in Overtown. These people came together and decided upon a list of priorities that ought to change as a result of social injustice. They acted on those things while seeking to maintain civil liberties that had been enacted through legislation and preventing, to a degree, the possibility of reprisals. The CRB served as advisor to the mayor, commissioners, and the county administration on issues impacting economic, social, and religious matters, as well as ethnic group relations in the county.

I got involved just before I became pastor of Sweet Home in 1983. I ended up becoming the board chair in 2011 and remained at the helm of the CRB until 2016. A person is only supposed to be on the board for no longer than eight years, so I am the longest serving member. I kept getting exceptions that would allow me to remain. The only reason I didn't remain on the CRB was because I could not be on two boards at the same time, as I became a member of the Public Health Trust for Jackson Health System in December 2016. During my time on the CRB, I was sort of the ears and eyes of the black community for its members, but I was also the mouthpiece for the black community to a county that was run by whites and Hispanics. I went to Jackson because I was requested by Al Dotson, who had been selected to be on that seven-member board.

Back when the Jackson Hospital board had 22 members, it was more diverse, but when they decreased the number to just seven members, they've never had more than one black member. Accomplished trial lawyer Larry Handfield had been the chair, and before that, once-prominent accountant Darryl Sharpton had been on the board the year prior. Thus, we've had a number of prominent blacks, but only one at a time. Before I got on the board, Al was on the board but found out that his law firm was doing business with Jackson. Because of the conflict of interest, he sought me out to finish his term. I took this appointment as an opportunity to continue my mission of making sure that blacks were treated fairly. I said to them that I was "honored" to be a part of a board where there was very little minority representation, including women. There were Hispanics on the board, but women and blacks were underrepresented. Even now, I'm the only black member on the board, and I have been able to help our community, including one family from my old neighborhood in Opa-locka.

Attorney Larry called me in February 2021 and said, "I have a client who has a situation that only you can help me with."

I said, "What's that?"

He said, "My client's sister is in the hospital at Jackson North, and they dropped her off because she was almost nonresponsive. She's developmentally disabled, so she's not able to communicate. They've not heard from the hospital about her condition in over a day, so I need you to get involved."

"No problem," I replied. "Give me the sister's name and give me a relative's name whom the hospital can get in contact with, and I'll check it out."

As soon as he gave me the name of the young lady and the name of her next-of-kin, I sensed a familiar connection. They were neighbors from my block in Opa-locka when I was growing up as a child. I called back Attorney Handfield and said, "Man, this is a friend of the family. This may be a client of yours, but this is like family to me. I'll jump right on this and I'll give you a call back."

I called the hospital and spoke with the CEO, saying, "Listen, I need you to tell me right away who's going to handle this and have them contact the family. Of course, you can't tell me what's happening medically, but you certainly need to call the family." I then added, "Listen, I know this about this family. They may not have told the hospital, but if you have her at a point where she can respond, don't call her by her name—call her 'Sister,' and you should get a response. That's her nickname."

As I had suggested, when they called her "Sister," she finally responded.

I called the brother, and I told him what I'd done. I said, "The hospital let me know that she responded once they called her 'Sister.'"

He said, "Wow, Walter, only you would think of something like that. Man, you've gone beyond. I didn't know you were on the board there. I would have called you instead of calling Larry had I known."

"So, what's the connection between you and Larry?" I inquired.

"Larry and I went to college together at Bethune-Cookman. His freshman year was my senior year, but we hit it off because we're both from Dade County."

The man I had helped was Nathaniel Jackson, one of 15 children, who had been raised in the same community. When they took his younger sister to the hospital, they ultimately learned that she had COVID-19 and wasn't able to communicate. Nathaniel had also contracted COVID, and so did his daughter. They had all been quarantined since the previous week but were doing well enough to avoid hospitalization. While they experienced some negative side effects, Sister succumbed to the virus. She was younger than I, closer to Alfred's age. None of us could or will ever forget her.

At times, I question whether I have outlived my usefulness, but situations like this remind me that I still have opportunities and the means to help our community. There's still more work to do, and whether people acknowledge my legacy in Christian music, ministry, community reform or social justice, I know the harvest is still plentiful. I shall continue to labor until I get tired, which is probably no time soon. Until then, my major mission is to make sure there's someone who can take my place among the others who have been fighting in the struggle for equality and social justice, and also prepare the next generation for the work that will undoubtedly be theirs once the elder generation is off the scene. My unofficial job, then, is to make sure that those who come behind me have the opportunity to glean and learn from my experiences in minority business, society, and politics. My prayer is that my contributions will become an inspiration so young people can move forward with more wisdom, understanding, and hope.

REFERENCES

About: Chapman Partnership. Chapman Partnership (2021, June 18). Retrieved April 14, 2021, from https://chapmanpartnership.org/about

Anderson, Paul. "Clinton Offers Hope to Rebuild Homestead Base." *The Miami Herald*. Feb. 12, 1993.

Bell, Maya. "We Were Hired to Kill Anti-Drug Crusader, 2 Say." *The Orlando Sentinel*. Apr 4, 1989. https://www.orlandosentinel.com/1989/04/04/we-were-hired-to-kill-anti-drug-crusader-2-say Accessed on 5/4/21

Benowitz, Shayne. "The History of Liberty Square." Greater Miami Convention & Visitors Bureau. July 22, 2020. https://www.miamiandbeaches.com/things-to-do/history-and-heritage/the-history-of-liberty-square

Clark, Chuck and Yanez, Luisa. "'Town Host, Clinton Pledges Fairness to All." *Sun-Sentinel*. February 11, 1993.

Cohen, Howard. "'Tri-county builder Harry Mursten of Mursten Construction dies at 85." *The Miami Herald*. August 3, 2016. Retrieved from https://www.miamiherald.com/news/local/community/broward/article93369547.html

"Conscientious Objectors." Selective Service System. Accessed on 10/14/21 https://www.sss.gov/conscientious-objectors/

Dellagloria, Rebecca. "Release of Killer Stuns Victim's Kin." *The Miami Herald*, Apr 7, 2008. Retrieved on 5/4/21 https://www.miamiherald.com/news/local/community/miami-dade/article1929118.html

Dickerson, Dennis C. 2016. "Our History." *AME Church.* November 06. Accessed 2021. https://www.ame-church.com/our-church/our-history

Hines, Bea L. "Bishop Walter H. Richardson dies at 100; was longtime pastor of Liberty City church." *The Miami Herald.* January 20, 2023. Retrieved from https://www.miamiherald.com/news/local/obituaries/article271373992.html

Jenkins Fields, Dorothy. "15 Historic Sites in Miami's Liberty City." Greater Miami Convention & Visitors Bureau. July 29, 2020. https://www.miamiandbeaches.com/things-to-do/history-and-heritage/15-historic-sites-in-miamis-liberty-city

Leonnig, Carol D. and Nakamura, David. "Secret Service scandal: Rising supervisor set uncovering of misconduct in motion." *Washington Post,* April 21, 2012. https://www.washingtonpost.com/politics/secret-service-scandal-rising-supervisor-at-heart-of-uncovering-misconduct/2012/04/21/gIQApy37XT_story.html

"President and His Faith — The Faith-Based Initiative Controversy." FRONTLINE: The Jesus Factor. Georgia Public Broadcasting (April 29, 2004). Retrieved May 12, 2021, from https://www.pbs.org/wgbh/pages/frontline/shows/jesus/president/faithbased.html

Saez, Emmanuel, and Gabriel Zucman. 2019. *The Triumph of Injustice: How the Rich Dodge Taxes and How to Make Them Pay.* University of California, Berkeley: W. W. Norton & Company.

San Martin, Nancy. "Haitian Issue Crystallizes Community." January 22, 1993. https://www.sun-sentinel.com/news/fl-xpm-1993-01-22-9301050089-story.html

Street, S.E., Morgan, T.J.H., Thornton, A. *et al.* Human mate-choice copying is domain-general social learning. *Sci Rep* 8, 1715 (2018). https://doi.org/10.1038/s41598-018-19770-8

The New Tropic Creative Studio. "Georgette's Tea Room: A historic meeting place for Miami's black arts community." The New Tropic.

June 20, 2019. https://thenewtropic.com/georgettes-tea-room-a-historic-meeting-place-for-miamis-black-arts-community/

Tinsley, Gigi. "Bishop Walter H. Richardson Leads with Everything." *Miami Times*. June 14, 2017. https://www.miamitimesonline.com/faith_family/family_news/bishop-walter-h-richardson-leads-with-everything/article_6aa160c6-511f-11e7-befa-2b8e90ee12e9.html

Viglucci, Andres. "NAACP Members begin fast in sympathy with Haitians." *The Miami Herald*, section 1B, Jan. 14, 1993.

www.ingramcontent.com/pod-product-compliance
Lightning Source LLC
Chambersburg PA
CBHW041929090426
42744CB00016B/1989